FABULOUS
FISH
IN MINUTES

FABULOUS
FISH
IN MINUTES

QUICK AND HEALTHY INSPIRATIONS
FOR EVERY MEAL

LINDA DOESER

Sebastian Kelly

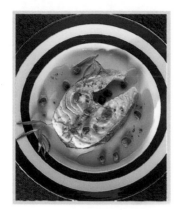

First published in 1998 by
Sebastian Kelly

© Anness Publishing Limited 1998

Produced by Anness Publishing Limited
Hermes House, 88-89 Blackfriars Road, London SE1 8HA

ISBN 1 84081 024 6

Publisher: Joanna Lorenz
Cookery Editor: Linda Doeser
Copy Editor: Leslie Viney
Designers: Mason Linklater, Siân Keogh
Illustrator: Madeleine David

Front Cover: Lisa Tai, Designer; Thomas Odulate, Photographer;
Helen Trent, Stylist; Marie-Ange Lapierre, Home Economist

Previously published as part of a larger compendium, *The Great Fish and Shellfish Cookbook*

Printed in Hong Kong/China

1 3 5 7 9 10 8 6 4 2

NOTES
All standard spoon and cup measurements are level.

CONTENTS

~

Introduction

Fish is the ultimate fast food—its delicate texture and flavor make it the perfect choice for preparing quick and easy meals. Most of the recipes in this book can be completed within twenty minutes and many of them take even less time.

The range of fish and seafood is immense, and the variety of ways in which it can be cooked is huge. Fast-cooked doesn't simply mean fried or broiled—although Pan-fried Garlic Sardines, Crumb-coated Shrimp, Fish Steaks with Mustard Sauce, and Grilled Green Mussels with Cumin are mouthwatering examples of these ways of cooking. Fish can also be poached, steamed, baked, deep-fried, curried, and made into filling stews. It goes well with most vegetables, pasta, cheese, many herbs and spices, and makes wonderful salads, and delicate soups. Its versatility is almost endless.

The recipes in this book are divided into four chapters. Soups & Appetizers includes traditional favorites, such as Clam Chowder, and some unusual appetizers, such as Sole Goujons with Lime Mayonnaise. The recipes in Fish Dishes range from Tuna and Corn Fish Cakes to Salmon with Green Peppercorns and from Sicilian Spaghetti with Sardines to Red Snapper with Cilantro Salsa— something to suit all tastes. Seafood Dishes includes a traditional Thai Green Shrimp Curry, Steamed Chili Mussels, Spicy Squid, and Linguine with Clams—all of them a veritable feast made in moments. Salads similarly demonstrates the variety and versatility of fish and seafood, with recipes ranging from Warm Salmon Salad to Melon and Crab Salad, and from Avocado and Smoked Fish Salad to Shrimp Salad with Curry Dressing. A helpful introductory section is packed with information about types of fish and seafood, buying and storing, and a step-by-step guide to some basic techniques. Hints and tips throughout provide further advice and information.

Types of Fish and Seafood

For the purposes of cooking, fish are usually divided into freshwater and sea fish and this second group is subdivided into round and flat fish. Seafood includes edible shellfish, crustaceans, squid, and octopus. Listed below are some of the most popular varieties.

Anchovy

Round fish, related to the herring family, anchovies are silvery and about 6 inches long. Fresh anchovies are not widely available. Canned anchovies are salt-cured. Whole salted anchovies are occasionally available.

Bonito

A round fish, related to the mackerel family, the silvery, striped bonito can grow as long as 3 feet. Fresh steaks and fillets are occasionally available, but the fish is most often sold in cans. Bonito flakes—shaved from the dried, smoked fish—are used in Japanese cuisine and are available from Asian supermarkets.

Clam

There are many varieties of this shellfish, ranging in size from 1–5 inches across. They are available fresh and bottled or canned in brine.

Cod

A round fish and the chief member of a large family that also includes haddock, hake, and whiting, cod can grow to 4 feet long. It is widely available as steaks, cutlets, and fillets. Whole young cod are sometimes sold. Nowadays, smoked cod is often cured and colored, rather than smoked in the traditional manner. Both types require further cooking. Salt cod is usually sold as fillets, but whole fish are sometimes available. It must be soaked for about 48 hours before cooking.

Crab

There are thousands of different varieties of this crustacean in a vast range of sizes and colors. Almost all have hard shells and many have a pair of large claws. Fresh crab can be bought both live and cooked. The flesh is often separated into brown meat from inside the shell, and white meat from the legs and claws. The pink coral from female crabs is regarded as a delicacy. Frozen and canned crab meat are widely available.

Dab

A member of the flat fish family that also includes lemon sole, plaice, and halibut, the rough-skinned dab ranges in size from 8 ounces–1½ pounds.

Dover sole

A flat fish, Dover sole is the fish used in many classic recipes. Lemon sole is quite different. The underside is white and the top surface is usually light brown. It is sold whole or in fillets.

Gurnard

A round fish, red gurnard is the most popular, but there are also yellow and gray varieties. Whole fish, weighing about 2¼ pounds, and steaks are available.

Haddock

A member of the cod family and also a North Atlantic fish, haddock is smaller than cod, reaching about 2 feet. It is usually sold as cutlets, steaks, or fillets. Traditionally, smoked haddock is available in fillets, which require further cooking. Finnan haddock is a whole fish soaked in brine before before being smoked.

Hake

A round fish, hake grows to about 2 feet long. It is mainly sold whole and as fillets. Steaks cut from especially large specimens are sometimes available.

Halibut

A very large flat fish, halibut is usually sold as steaks or fillets. Smoked halibut is available as a whole side or thinly sliced, and it requires no further cooking.

Herring

A round, silvery fish with a high oil content, herring grows to about 10 inches long. It is available whole and as fillets. Smoked herring, in the form of kippers, is widely available, sold whole or in fillets. It may be eaten with no further cooking, marinated, boiled or poached.

Lemon sole

A fairly large flat fish with a mottled top surface and a pale underside, lemon sole is different from Dover sole. Smaller fish are usually sold whole and larger ones are available whole and as fillets.

Mackerel

An iridescent blue-gray round fish, mackerel is usually sold whole. It weighs up to 1½ pounds. Smoked mackerel is widely available whole or in fillets. It may be eaten without further cooking.

Monkfish
A round fish, it is rarely sold whole, not least because of its extremely ugly, large head. It is usually sold as monkfish tail, weighing 1½–3 pounds. This is often skinned, but is usually still covered with a tough, transparent membrane that must be removed before cooking or it will shrink and toughen.

Mussel
This shellfish varies considerably in size and the shells may be deep blue, black, brown or green-lipped. Live fresh mussels are widely available and they are also sold frozen and canned.

Plaice
A flat fish, it is easily distinguished by orange spots on the upper surface. It grows to about 18 inches long and is sold whole or in fillets.

Red mullet
A round fish, red mullet is available in two varieties. The redder and sweeter-tasting type is sometimes known as golden mullet. It is usually sold whole.

Salmon
A round freshwater fish, salmon migrates to the sea to feed before returning to rivers to spawn. Fresh salmon is usually the Atlantic variety and it may be sold whole, in steaks, cutlets, or fillets. It is now widely farmed, which produces fish with a softer texture and less flavor. Wild salmon is available in season. Pacific and Alaskan salmon are usually canned. Smoked salmon is widely available as a whole side or in slices. It is usually eaten with no further cooking. Cured salmon is sold thinly sliced.

Salmon trout
A round fish, also known as sea trout, this is a freshwater fish that migrates to the sea to feed before returning to fresh water to spawn. It closely resembles brown trout in appearance. Smoked salmon trout is increasingly available as a whole side or in slices. It requires no further cooking.

Sardine
Sardines are actually young pilchards: thin, silvery fish weighing about 4 ounces. They have a mass of fine scales that should be gently scraped off with your hand under cold running water before cooking. They are widely available canned in oil.

Scallop
A fan-shaped shellfish, the scallop ranges in size from 3–7 inches across. There are many different varieties and they are available in their shells and shelled, fresh or frozen. The orange-colored coral or roe is regarded as a delicacy.

Sea bass
A dark gray round fish that may weigh as much as 20 pounds and grow as long as 3 feet, it is most often sold and cooked whole. The spiny dorsal fin and the scales must be removed before cooking.

Sea bream
This comprises a family of round fish, which vary in color from dark gray through light gray to crimson. The last variety is also known as red porgy. It is quite different from and much better flavored than freshwater bream. It is usually sold whole, weighing about 2 pounds, but fillets are occasionally available.

Shrimp
This family of crustaceans ranges in size from about 2–9 inches, and in color from blue through pink to brown. Shrimp are available raw and cooked, fresh and frozen.

Snapper
This comprises a family of round fish, varying in size from 6 inches–3 feet, and in color from red through orange to pink. It is available whole and in fillets.

Squid
Classed as seafood, squid is a member of the octopus family. It ranges in size from 2–10 inches. It is available whole and ready-prepared, fresh and frozen.

Trout
There are two varieties of this round, freshwater fish—brown and rainbow. Brown trout are about 12 inches long and thought to have the better flavor, but may be difficult to obtain. Rainbow trout are iridescent with pink flesh. They are extensively farmed and usually sold whole or in fillets. Smoked trout is also widely available as whole fish and in fillets. It needs no further cooking.

Tuna
A round fish of the mackerel family, tuna ranges in size from about 2½ pounds to over 1,000 pounds. Fresh tuna is usually sold as steaks. It is widely available canned in oil or brine.

Whitebait
These tiny round fish, the young of herring, sprats, and sometimes of other fish, are about 2 inches long. They are invariably sold and cooked whole.

Buying and Storing

A shining skin, bright color, pink gills, and full bright eyes with black pupils and transparent corneas are the signs of fresh fish. The body should feel firm and springy. It should have clean, pleasant smell, not a nasty "fishy" odor. The scales should be clearly in place.

Shellfish deteriorates very quickly, so if it is not fresh, your nose will inform you immediately.

Many types of shellfish, such as clams and mussels, are sold live to ensure freshness. Crab may also be sold live and is available ready-cooked. When preparing live mussels, clams, or other shellfish, discard any that have damaged shells or that do not close at once when sharply tapped with the back of a knife. These are already dead and will contaminate the dish.

Discard any that have not opened by the end of cooking.

Ideally, fish should be cooked and eaten on the day of purchase. It may be stored in the refrigerator for a maximum of one day. Wrap it loosely in wax paper or foil to prevent its smell penetrating other foods. If not alive, seafood should always be cooked and eaten on the day of purchase.

Poaching

Whole fish, large and small, as well as fillets, cutlets and steaks, are excellent poached because the gentle cooking gives succulent results. Poached fish can be served hot or cold with a wide variety of sauces. The poaching liquid may be used as a basis for the sauce.

1 To oven poach small, whole fish, fillets, cutlets or steaks, place the fish in a buttered, flame-proof dish that is large enough to hold the pieces in a single layer. Pour in enough liquid to come two-thirds of the way up the sides of the fish.

2 Add any flavorings specified in the recipe. Press a piece of buttered waxed paper on top to keep in the moisture.

3 Set the dish over medium heat and bring the liquid just to a boil. Transfer the dish to a pre-heated oven at 350°F and poach until the fish is just cooked. To test, with the tip of a sharp knife, make a small cut into the thickest part of the fish, ideally near a bone. The flesh should be slightly translucent.

4 To poach whole fish, fillets, cutlets or steaks on the stove, put large whole fish on the rack in a fish kettle or set on a piece of muslin that can be used like a hammock. Small whole fish, fillets, cutlets and steaks may be poached in a fish kettle on a rack or set directly in a wide saucepan or frying pan.

5 Prepare the poaching liquid—water, milk, wine or stock—in the fish kettle, a large casserole, a roasting pan, a wide saucepan or frying pan, as appropriate. Set the rack in the kettle or the muslin hammock in the casserole or pan. Add more liquid if necessary.

6 Cover the kettle or casserole and bring the liquid just to a boil. Reduce the heat and simmer very gently until the fish is cooked.

Steaming

This simple, moist-heat method of cooking is ideal for fish and shellfish. If you do not have a steamer, it is easy to improvise.

1 Using a steamer, arrange the fish on the steamer rack and set over boiling water. Cover and steam until done.

2 For Chinese-style steaming, arrange the fish on a heatproof plate that will fit inside a bamboo steamer or wok. Put the plate in the steamer or on the rack in the wok, set over boiling water, cover and steam until done.

3 For steaming larger fish and fillets, arrange the fish on a rack in a roasting pan of boiling water or on a plate set on the rack. Cover tightly with foil and steam until done.

4 To steam in foil, wrap the fish and seasonings in foil, sealing well, and set on a rack in the steamer or in a large roasting pan of boiling water. Steam until done.

Broiling

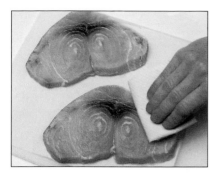

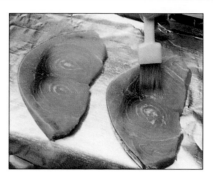

1 To broil small, whole oily fish, boned and butterflied fish, fillets, cutlets and steaks that are at least ½ inch thick or cubes of fish on skewers, rinse the fish and pat it dry with paper towels. Marinate the fish if the recipe suggests this.

2 Preheat the broiler with the broiler pan in place. When hot, lightly brush the hot pan with oil. Arrange the fish in the pan in a single layer, skin side down, brush the fish with butter, oil or a basting mixture, according to the recipe.

3 Set the fish under the broiler, 3–4 inches from the heat. Thin pieces should be closer to the heat for a shorter time than thicker ones. Broil, basting once or twice and turning if the recipe specifies, until the fish is done.

4 To broil leaner, small whole fish, steaks, cutlets and fillets that are at least ½ inch thick and prepared for cooking as above, arrange in a buttered, flameproof dish. Add a little liquid—wine, stock or court bouillon—just to cover the base of the dish. Brush the fish with butter, oil or a basting mixture, according to the recipe. Broil as above, without turning the fish.

Coating and Frying

1 Lightly beat an egg in a shallow dish. Spread some flour on a plate or sheet of waxed paper and season with salt and freshly ground black pepper or ingredients as specified in the recipe. Spread fine bread crumbs or crushed crackers on another plate or sheet of waxed paper.

2 To egg and crumb large pieces of fish, dip the fish first in the seasoned flour, turning to coat both sides lightly and evenly. Shake or brush off excess flour.

3 Next, dip the floured fish in the egg, turning to moisten both sides.

4 Dip the fish in the crumbs, turning to coat evenly. Press to help the crumbs adhere. Shake or pat off excess crumbs. Chill for at least 20 minutes to set the coating.

5 To egg and crumb small pieces of fish, strips of fish fillet or shrimp, put the crumbs in a plastic bag. After dipping the fish in seasoned flour and egg, toss a few pieces at a time in the plastic bag of crumbs.

6 To pan fry, heat some oil or a mixture of oil and butter in a frying pan, using enough to coat the base of the pan in a thin layer or according to recipe instructions. When it is very hot, put the fish in the pan in a single layer. Fry until golden brown on both sides and the fish is done. Drain on kitchen paper before serving.

7 To deep-fry, half fill a deep pan with oil and heat it to 375°F. Gently lower the coated pieces of fish into the hot oil, frying them only a few at a time. Fry until golden brown, turning them occasionally, so that they cook evenly. Remove and drain thoroughly on paper towels before serving.

SOUPS &
APPETIZERS

~

Corn and Crab Meat Soup

This soup originated in the United States, but it has since been introduced into China. You must use creamed corn in the recipe to achieve the right consistency.

Serves 4

4 ounces crab meat or chicken breast
2 teaspoons finely chopped fresh ginger
2 egg whites
2 tablespoons milk
1 tablespoon cornstarch paste
2½ cups vegetable or chicken stock
1 can (8 ounces) creamed corn
salt and freshly ground black pepper
finely chopped scallions, to garnish

1 Flake the crab meat (or roughly chop the chicken breast) and mix with the ginger.

2 Beat the egg whites until frothy, add the milk and cornstarch paste and beat again until smooth. Blend with the crab meat or chicken breast.

3 In a wok or saucepan, bring the stock to a boil, then add the creamed corn and bring back to a boil.

4 Stir in the crab meat or chicken breast and egg-white mixture, adjust the seasonings to taste and stir gently until well blended and the meat is cooked. Serve garnished with finely chopped scallions.

Crab and Egg Noodle Broth

This delicious broth is the perfect solution when you are hungry, time is short, and you need something fast, nutritious and filling.

INGREDIENTS

Serves 4

4 ounces fine egg noodles

2 tablespoons unsalted butter

1 small bunch scallions, chopped

1 celery stalk, sliced

1 medium carrot, peeled and cut
   into batons

5 cups chicken stock

¼ cup dry sherry

4 ounces white crab meat, fresh or frozen

pinch of celery salt

pinch of cayenne pepper

2 teaspoons lemon juice

1 small bunch cilantro or flat leaf parsley,
   to garnish

3 Add the chicken stock and sherry to the pan, bring to a boil, reduce the heat and simmer for another 5 minutes.

4 If using frozen crab meat, let it thaw. Flake the crab meat between your fingers onto a plate and remove any stray pieces of shell.

5 Drain the noodles and add to the broth, together with the crab meat. Season to taste with celery salt and cayenne pepper and sharpen with the lemon juice. Return to a simmer.

6 Ladle the broth into shallow soup plates, scatter with roughly chopped cilantro to garnish and serve.

1 Bring a large saucepan of water to a boil. Toss in the egg noodles and cook according to the instructions on the package. Cool under cold running water, drain and leave immersed in water until required.

2 Heat the butter in another large pan, add the scallions, celery and carrot, cover and soften the vegetables over low heat for 3–4 minutes.

Clam Chowder

*Clams canned or bottled in brine
can be used instead of fresh ones.*

Serves 4

1¼ cups heavy cream

6 tablespoons sweet butter

1 small onion, finely chopped

1 apple, sliced

1 garlic clove, crushed

3 tablespoons mild curry powder

12 ounces baby corn

2½ cups fish stock

8 ounces new potatoes, peeled and cooked

24 baby onions, peeled and boiled

40 small fresh clams

salt and freshly ground black pepper

8 lime wedges, to garnish

1 Pour the cream into a small saucepan and cook over a high heat until it is reduced by half.

2 Melt half the butter in another pan. Sauté the onion, apple, garlic, and curry powder over a low heat until the onion is translucent but not colored. Stir in the reduced cream.

3 Melt the remaining butter in another saucepan. Add the baby corn and cook for 5 minutes. Increase the heat and add the cream and onion mixture and stock. Bring to a boil.

4 Add the potatoes, baby onions, and clams. Cover and cook until the clams have opened. Discard any that do not open. Season well to taste and serve, garnished with the lime wedges.

Seafood Soup with Rouille

This is a really chunky aromatic mixed fish soup from Provence, France, flavored with plenty of saffron and herbs. Rouille, a fiery hot paste, is served separately for everyone to swirl into their soup to flavor. It means rust, which describes its red color resulting from the chili and bell pepper. Saffron is also sometimes included.

INGREDIENTS

Serves 6

3 gurnard or red mullet, filleted

12 large raw or cooked shrimp

1½ pounds white fish fillets, such as cod, haddock, halibut, or monkfish

8 ounces fresh mussels

1 teaspoon saffron strands

1 tablespoon boiling water

5 tablespoons olive oil

1 fennel bulb, roughly chopped

4 garlic cloves, crushed

3 strips orange rind

4 thyme sprigs

5 cups fish stock

14-ounce can chopped tomatoes

2 tablespoons sun-dried tomato paste

3 bay leaves

salt and freshly ground black pepper

For the rouille

1 red bell pepper, seeded and roughly chopped

1 red chili, seeded and sliced

2 garlic cloves, chopped

5 tablespoons olive oil

¼ cup fresh bread crumbs

1 First make the rouille. Put the bell pepper, chili, garlic, oil, and bread crumbs in a blender or food processor and process until smooth. Transfer the rouille to a serving dish and chill in the refrigerator until required.

2 Cut the gurnard or red mullet fillets into large chunks. Peel half the shrimp. Skin the white fish fillets, remove any remaining bones, and cut the flesh into large chunks. Debeard and scrub the mussels well under cold running water, discarding any damaged ones and any that do not close immediately when tapped sharply with the back of a knife.

3 Soak the saffron strands in the boiling water. Meanwhile, heat 2 tablespoons of the olive oil in a large sauté pan or saucepan. Add the gurnard or mullet and white fish chunks and fry over a high heat for 1 minute. Remove from the pan and drain.

4 Add the remaining oil to the pan and return to the heat. Add the fennel, garlic, orange rind, and thyme and fry, stirring from time to time, until beginning to color.

5 Add the stock to the pan, together with the saffron liquid, tomatoes, sun-dried tomato paste, and bay leaves. Season to taste with salt and pepper. Bring almost to a boil, lower the heat, cover, and simmer for 15 minutes.

6 Stir in the gurnard or mullet chunks, white fish chunks, peeled and unpeeled shrimp, and the mussels. Cover and cook for 3–4 minutes. Discard any mussels that do not open. Serve the soup hot with the rouille.

COOK'S TIP

If you prefer a milder-tasting accompaniment, substitute the equally authentic Provençal paste called pistou. This is very similar to Italian pesto. Skin and seed 2 very ripe, large tomatoes and roughly chop the flesh. Pound together the tomato flesh, 5 garlic cloves, 4 tablespoons fresh basil leaves and 1 cup freshly grated Parmesan cheese in a mortar with a pestle. Transfer to a bowl and gradually beat in 4 tablespoons olive oil until fully incorporated. Alternatively, process the tomatoes, garlic, basil, and cheese in a food processor until smooth. With the motor still running, gradually add the olive oil. Stir the pistou into the soup before serving or hand round separately.

Deep-fried Whitebait

A spicy coating on these fish gives this favorite dish a crunchy bite.

INGREDIENTS

Serves 6

1 cup flour
½ teaspoon curry powder
½ teaspoon ground ginger
½ teaspoon ground cayenne pepper
pinch of salt
2½ pounds fresh or frozen
 whitebait, thawed
vegetable oil, for deep-frying
lemon wedges, to garnish

1 Combine the flour, spices and salt in a large bowl.

2 Coat the fish in the seasoned flour and shake off any excess.

3 Heat the oil in a large heavy saucepan until it reaches a temperature of 375°F. Fry the whitebait in batches for 2–3 minutes until the fish is golden and crispy.

4 Drain well on absorbent paper towels. Serve hot, garnished with lemon wedges.

Smoked Salmon Crêpes with Pesto

These simple crêpes take no more than 10–15 minutes to prepare and are perfect for a special occasion. Smoked salmon is delicious with fresh basil and combines well with toasted pine nuts and a spoonful of crème fraîche.

INGREDIENTS

Makes 12–16

½ cup milk

1 cup self-rising flour

1 egg

2 tablespoons pesto sauce

vegetable oil, for frying

scant 1 cup crème fraîche

4 ounces smoked salmon

¼ cup pine nuts, toasted

salt and freshly ground black pepper

12–16 fresh basil sprigs, to garnish

3 Heat the vegetable oil in a large frying pan. Spoon the crêpe mixture into the heated oil in small heaps. Allow about 30 seconds for the crêpes to rise, then turn and cook briefly on the other side. Keep warm. Continue cooking the crêpes in batches until all the batter has been used up.

4 Arrange the crêpes on a serving plate and top each one with a spoonful of crème fraîche.

5 Cut the salmon into ½-inch strips and place on top of each crêpe. Scatter each crêpe with pine nuts and garnish with a sprig of fresh basil.

1 Pour half of the milk into a mixing bowl. Add the flour, egg, pesto sauce and seasoning and mix to a smooth batter.

2 Add the remainder of the milk and stir until evenly blended.

Sautéed Scallops

Scallops go well with all sorts of sauces, but simple cooking is the best way to enjoy their flavor.

INGREDIENTS

Serves 2

1 pound shelled scallops

2 tablespoons butter

2 tablespoons dry white vermouth

1 tablespoon finely chopped fresh parsley

salt and freshly ground black pepper

1 Rinse the scallops under cold running water to remove any sand or grit and pat dry using paper towels. Season them lightly with salt and pepper.

2 In a frying pan large enough to hold the scallops in one layer, heat half the butter until it begins to color. Sauté the scallops for 3–5 minutes, turning, until golden brown on both sides and just firm to the touch. Remove to a serving platter and cover to keep warm.

3 Add the vermouth to the hot frying pan, swirl in the remaining butter, add the parsley and pour the sauce over the scallops. Serve immediately.

Garlicky Scallops and Shrimp

Scallops and shrimp are found all along the Atlantic and Mediterranean coasts of France and are enjoyed in every region. This method of cooking is a typical Provençal recipe.

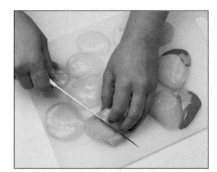

INGREDIENTS

Serves 2–4

6 large shelled scallops

6–8 large raw shrimp, peeled

flour, for dusting

2–3 tablespoons olive oil

1 garlic clove, finely chopped

1 tablespoon chopped fresh basil

2–3 tablespoons lemon juice

salt and freshly ground black pepper

1 Rinse the scallops under cold running water to remove any sand or grit. Pat them dry using paper towels and cut in half horizontally. Season the scallops and shrimp with salt and pepper and dust lightly with flour, shaking off the excess.

2 Heat the oil in a large frying pan over a high heat and add the scallops and shrimp.

3 Reduce the heat to medium-high and cook for 2 minutes, then turn the scallops and shrimp. Add the garlic and basil, shaking the pan to distribute them evenly. Cook for another 2 minutes until the scallops are golden and just firm to the touch. Sprinkle on the lemon juice and toss to blend.

VARIATION

To make a richer sauce, transfer the cooked scallops and shrimp to a warmed plate. Pour ¼ cup dry white wine into the frying pan and boil to reduce by half. Add 1 tablespoon unsalted butter, whisking until it melts and the sauce thickens slightly. Pour the sauce over the scallops and shrimp and serve.

Grilled Green Mussels with Cumin

Green-shelled mussels have a more distinctive flavor than the small, black variety. Keep the empty shells to use as individual salt and pepper holders for fishy meals.

INGREDIENTS

Serves 4

3 tablespoons fresh parsley

3 tablespoons fresh cilantro

1 garlic clove, crushed

pinch of ground cumin

2 tablespoons unsalted butter, softened

¼ cup brown bread crumbs

12 green mussels or 24 small mussels, on the half shell

freshly ground black pepper

chopped fresh parsley, to garnish

1 Finely chop the fresh parsley and cilantro.

2 Beat the garlic, herbs, cumin and butter together with a wooden spoon.

3 Stir in the bread crumbs and freshly ground black pepper.

4 Spoon a little of the mixture onto each mussel and grill for 2 minutes. Serve garnished with chopped fresh parsley.

Glazed Garlic Shrimp

This is a fairly simple and quick dish to prepare. It is best to peel the shrimp, as this helps them to absorb maximum flavor. Serve with a salad as an appetizer or as a main course with a selection of vegetables and other accompaniments.

INGREDIENTS

Serves 4

1 tablespoon vegetable oil

3 garlic cloves, roughly chopped

3 tomatoes, chopped

½ teaspoon salt

1 teaspoon crushed dried red chilies

1 teaspoon lemon juice

1 tablespoon mango chutney

1 fresh green chili, chopped

15–20 cooked jumbo shrimp, peeled
and deveined

fresh cilantro sprigs, 4 unpeeled, cooked
jumbo shrimp and 2 scallions, chopped,
to garnish

1 In a medium saucepan, heat the oil and add the chopped garlic cloves.

2 Lower the heat and add the chopped tomatoes along with the salt, crushed chilies, lemon juice, mango chutney and chopped fresh chili.

3 Finally, add the shrimp, turn up the heat and stir-fry them quickly, until heated through.

4 Transfer to a warmed serving dish. Serve garnished with fresh cilantro sprigs, unpeeled jumbo shrimp and chopped scallions, if desired.

COOK'S TIP

This is a very fiery dish—if you would prefer it less hot, carefully seed the chili before chopping and reduce the crushed chilies to a pinch.

Sole Goujons with Lime Mayonnaise

This simple dish can be rustled up very quickly. It also makes an excellent light lunch or supper.

INGREDIENTS

Serves 4

scant 1 cup mayonnaise

1 small garlic clove, crushed

2 teaspoons capers, rinsed and chopped

2 teaspoons chopped gherkins

grated rind and juice of 1 lime

1 tablespoon finely chopped
    fresh cilantro

1½ pounds sole fillets, skinned

2 eggs, beaten

2 cups fresh white bread crumbs

oil, for deep-frying

salt and freshly ground black pepper

lime wedges, to serve

1 To make the lime mayonnaise, combine the mayonnaise, garlic, capers, gherkins, lime rind and juice and chopped cilantro. Season with salt and pepper to taste. Transfer to a serving bowl and chill until required.

2 Cut the sole fillets into finger-length strips. Dip each strip first into the beaten egg, then into the bread crumbs.

3 Heat the oil in a deep-fat fryer to 350°F. Add the fish strips, in batches, and fry until they are golden brown and crisp. Drain well on paper towels and keep warm while you cook the remaining strips.

4 Pile the goujons onto warmed serving plates and serve with the lime wedges for squeezing lime juice onto them. Hand the sauce around separately.

Spicy Fish Rösti

You can also serve these fish cakes crisp and hot for lunch or supper with a mixed green salad.

INGREDIENTS

Serves 4

12 ounces large, firm waxy potatoes

12 ounces salmon or cod fillet, skinned
    and boned

3–4 scallions, finely chopped

1 teaspoon grated fresh ginger

2 tablespoons chopped fresh cilantro

2 teaspoons lemon juice

2–3 tablespoons sunflower oil

salt and cayenne pepper

cilantro sprigs, to garnish

lemon wedges, to serve

1 Cook the potatoes with their skins on in a pan of boiling salted water for 10 minutes. Drain and let cool for a few minutes.

2 Meanwhile, finely chop the salmon and put it into a bowl. Stir in the chopped scallions, grated ginger, chopped cilantro and lemon juice. Season to taste with salt and cayenne pepper.

3 When the potatoes are cool enough to handle, peel off the skins and grate the potatoes coarsely. Gently stir the grated potato into the fish mixture.

4 Form the fish mixture into 12 cakes, pressing the mixture together and leaving the edges slightly rough.

5 Heat the oil in a large frying pan and fry the fish cakes, a few at a time, for 3 minutes on each side, until golden brown and crisp. Drain on paper towels. Serve hot, garnished with sprigs of cilantro and with lemon wedges for squeezing the juice on top.

Welsh Rarebit with Anchovies

This classic snack or appetizer has been adapted and updated to include salty anchovies.

| INGREDIENTS |

Serves 4

1 can (2 ounces) canned anchovies,
   drained

12 tablespoons (1½ sticks) butter

6 slices of bread, crusts removed

4 large egg yolks

1¼ cups heavy cream

pinch of cayenne pepper

salt and freshly ground black pepper

1 tablespoon chopped fresh parsley,
   to garnish

1 In a food processor fitted with a metal blade, process the anchovy fillets with two-thirds of the butter. Toast the bread, spread with the anchovy butter, set aside and keep warm.

COOK'S TIP
〜

If you find canned anchovies too salty, soak them briefly in cold water before processing them with the butter.

2 Melt the remaining butter in a small heavy saucepan and beat in the egg yolks.

3 Take off the heat and add the cream. Season to taste, then replace on a low heat. Stir until the sauce is thick. Pour onto the toast and sprinkle with the cayenne pepper. Garnish with the chopped fresh parsley.

Seafood Wontons with Cilantro Dressing

These tasty wontons resemble tortellini. Water chestnuts add a light crunch to the filling.

INGREDIENTS

Serves 4

8 ounces cooked shrimp, peeled
   and deveined
4 ounces white crab meat
4 canned water chestnuts, finely diced
1 scallion, finely chopped
1 small green chili, seeded and
   finely chopped
¼ teaspoon grated fresh ginger
1 egg, separated
20–24 wonton wrappers
salt and freshly ground black pepper
cilantro leaves, to garnish

For the cilantro dressing
2 tablespoons rice vinegar
1 tablespoon chopped, pickled ginger
6 tablespoons olive oil
1 tablespoon soy sauce
3 tablespoons chopped cilantro
2 tablespoons finely diced red bell pepper

1 Finely dice the shrimp and place them in a bowl. Add the crab meat, water chestnuts, scallion, chili, ginger and egg white. Season with salt and pepper to taste and stir well.

2 Place a wonton wrapper on a board. Put about 1 teaspoon of the filling just above the center of the wrapper. With a pastry brush, moisten the edges of the wrapper with a little beaten egg yolk. Bring the bottom of the wrapper up over the filling. Press gently to expel any air, then seal the wrapper neatly in a triangle.

3 For a more elaborate shape, bring the two side points up over the filling, overlap the points and pinch the ends firmly together. Space the filled wontons an inch apart on a large baking sheet lined with waxed paper, so that they do not stick together.

4 Half fill a large saucepan with water. Bring to simmering point. Add the filled wontons, a few at a time, and simmer for 2–3 minutes or until the wontons float to the surface. When ready, the wrappers will be translucent and the filling should be cooked. Remove the wontons with a large slotted spoon, drain them briefly, then spread them on trays. Keep warm while you cook the remaining wontons.

5 Make the cilantro dressing by whisking all the ingredients together in a bowl. Divide the wontons among serving dishes, drizzle with the dressing and serve, garnished with a handful of cilantro leaves.

FISH
DISHES

~

Hoki Balls in Tomato Sauce

This quick meal is a good choice for young children, as you can guarantee no bones. Its low fat content also makes it an ideal dish for anyone on a low-fat or low-cholesterol diet. If desired, add a dash of chili sauce.

INGREDIENTS

Serves 4

1 pound hoki or other white fish
    fillets, skinned
¼ cup fresh whole wheat bread crumbs
2 tablespoons snipped chives or scallions
1 can (14 ounces) chopped tomatoes
2 ounces button mushrooms, sliced
salt and freshly ground black pepper
fresh chives, to garnish

1 Cut the fish fillets into large chunks and place in a food processor. Add the whole wheat bread crumbs and the chives or scallions. Season to taste with salt and pepper and process until the fish is finely chopped, but still has some texture left.

COOK'S TIP

Hoki is a good choice for this dish, but if it is not available, use cod, haddock or whiting instead.

2 Divide the fish mixture into about 16 even-size pieces, then mold them into balls with your hands.

3 Place the tomatoes and mushrooms in a large saucepan and cook over medium heat until boiling. Carefully add the fish balls, cover and simmer for about 10 minutes, until cooked. Serve hot, garnished with chives.

Cod with Caper Sauce

This quick and easy sauce, with a slightly sharp and nutty flavor, is a very effective way of enhancing a rather bland fish.

INGREDIENTS

Serves 4

4 cod steaks, about 6 ounces each

8 tablespoons (1 stick) butter

1 tablespoon vinegar

1 tablespoon capers

1 tablespoon chopped fresh parsley

salt and freshly ground black pepper

tarragon sprigs, to garnish

1 Season the cod with salt and pepper. Melt 2 tablespoons of the butter, then brush some over one side of each piece of cod.

2 Cook the cod in a preheated oven for about 6 minutes, turn it over, brush with more melted butter and cook for another 5–6 minutes or until the fish flakes easily.

3 Meanwhile, heat the remaining butter until it turns golden brown, but do not let it burn. Add the vinegar, followed by the capers, and stir well.

4 Pour the vinegar, butter and capers over the fish, sprinkle with parsley and garnish with the tarragon sprigs.

COOK'S TIP

Thick tail fillets of cod or haddock could be used in place of the cod steaks, if desired.

Breaded Fish with Tartar Sauce

All the taste of the classic fish dish but without any frying.

Serves 4

½ cup dried bread crumbs

1 teaspoon dried oregano

½ teaspoon cayenne pepper

1 cup milk

4 pieces of cod fillet, about 1½ pounds

3 tablespoons butter or margarine, melted

salt

For the tartar sauce

½ cup mayonnaise

½ teaspoon Dijon mustard

1–2 pickled gherkins, finely chopped

1 tablespoon drained capers, chopped

1 teaspoon chopped fresh parsley

1 teaspoon chopped fresh chives

1 teaspoon chopped fresh tarragon

salt and freshly ground black pepper

2 Dip the pieces of cod fillet in the milk, then transfer to the plate and coat with the bread crumb mixture.

3 Arrange the coated fish in the prepared baking dish, in a single layer. Drizzle the melted butter over the fish.

4 Bake in the center of the oven at 450°F for 10–15 minutes, until the fish flakes easily when tested with a fork.

5 Meanwhile, combine all the ingredients for the tartar sauce in a small bowl. Stir gently to mix thoroughly. Serve the fish hot, accompanied by the tartar sauce, passed separately.

1 Grease a shallow ovenproof baking dish. Combine the bread crumbs, oregano and cayenne pepper on a plate and blend together. Mix the milk with 2 teaspoons salt in a bowl, stirring well to dissolve the salt.

Chunky Fish Balti with Bell Peppers

Try to find as many differently colored sweet peppers as possible to make this very attractive dish.

INGREDIENTS

Serves 2–4

1 pound cod, or any other firm white fish

1½ teaspoons ground cumin

2 teaspoons mango powder

1 teaspoon ground coriander

½ teaspoon chili powder

1 teaspoon ginger pulp

3 tablespoons cornstarch

⅔ cup corn oil

3 colored bell peppers, seeded and chopped

salt

8–10 cherry tomatoes, to garnish

1 Skin the fish and cut it into small cubes. Put the fish cubes into a large mixing bowl and add the ground cumin, mango powder, ground coriander, chili powder, 1 teaspoon salt, ginger pulp and cornstarch. Combine thoroughly, using 2 spoons or your hands, until the fish is well coated.

2 Heat the oil in a preheated wok or karahi. Lower the heat and add the fish pieces, 3 or 4 at a time. Fry for about 3 minutes, turning and moving them constantly.

3 Drain the fish on paper towels. Transfer to a serving dish and keep warm while you fry the remaining fish pieces.

4 Add the peppers to the wok or karahi and fry for 2 minutes. They should still be slightly crisp. Drain on paper towels.

5 Add the drained peppers to the serving dish and garnish with the cherry tomatoes. Serve immediately.

Fried Fish with Piquant Mayonnaise

This sauce makes fried fish just that extra bit special and is very quick to prepare and cook, too.

INGREDIENTS

Serves 4

1 egg

3 tablespoons olive oil

squeeze of lemon juice

½ teaspoon finely chopped fresh dill
   or parsley

4 whiting or haddock fillets

flour, for dusting

2 tablespoons butter or margarine

salt and freshly ground black pepper

mixed salad, to serve

For the mayonnaise

1 egg yolk

2 tablespoons Dijon mustard

2 tablespoons white wine vinegar

2 teaspoons paprika

1¼ cups olive or vegetable oil

2 tablespoons creamed horseradish

1 garlic clove, finely chopped

½ stalk celery, finely chopped

2 tablespoons ketchup

1 To make the mayonnaise, blend the egg yolk, mustard, vinegar and paprika in a mixing bowl. Add the oil in a thin stream, beating vigorously with a wire whisk to blend it in.

2 When the mixture is smooth and thick, beat in all the other mayonnaise ingredients. Cover and chill until ready to serve.

3 Combine the egg, 1 tablespoon of the olive oil, the lemon juice, the dill or parsley and a little salt and pepper in a shallow dish. Beat until well mixed.

4 Dip both sides of each fish fillet in the egg and herb mixture, then coat the fillets lightly and evenly with flour, shaking off the excess.

5 Heat the butter with the remaining olive oil in a large heavy frying pan. Fry the coated fish fillets for 8–10 minutes, until golden brown on both sides and cooked through. If necessary, cook the fish in two batches, keeping the cooked fish warm while you are cooking the remainder.

6 Serve the fish hot, with the piquant mayonnaise and accompanied by a salad.

Haddock and Broccoli Stew

This is an easy, one-pot meal full of color and texture.

INGREDIENTS

Serves 4

4 scallions, sliced

1 pound new potatoes, diced

1¼ cups fish stock or water

1¼ cups milk

1 bay leaf

½ bunch broccoli florets, sliced

1 pound smoked haddock fillets, skinned

1 can (7 ounces) corn, drained

freshly ground black pepper

chopped scallions, to garnish

crusty bread, to serve

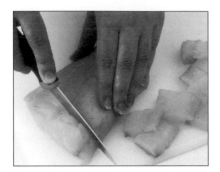

1 Place the scallions and potatoes in a large saucepan and add the stock or water, milk and bay leaf. Bring the mixture to a boil, then cover the pan and simmer for 10 minutes.

2 Add the broccoli to the pan. Cut the fish into bite-size chunks and add to the pan with the corn.

3 Season the stew well with freshly ground black pepper, then cover the pan and simmer for another 5 minutes or until the fish is cooked through. Remove the bay leaf and transfer to a serving dish. Scatter on the scallions and serve hot with crusty bread.

COOK'S TIP

When new potatoes are not available, old ones can be used, but choose a waxy variety that will not disintegrate.

Haddock with Leek Sauté

Instead of the classic cheese sauce, this Swiss cheese-topped leek sauté allows the fresh taste of the haddock fillet to dominate. Garnish with long chives for this clever lattice effect.

Serves 4

4 x 8 ounces haddock fillets

1½ pounds leeks

1 onion

2 tablespoons butter

1 teaspoon caraway seeds

½ cup finely grated Swiss cheese

salt and freshly ground black pepper

long chives, to garnish (optional)

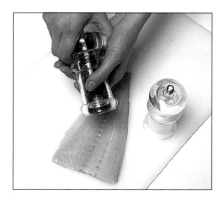

1 Season the fish with salt and pepper. Preheat the broiler.

2 With a sharp knife, cut the leeks into ½-inch thick diagonal slices. Coarsely chop the onion.

3 Melt the butter in a large, heavy-based saucepan and sauté the leeks and onion until soft. Stir in the caraway seeds.

4 Line the base of a flameproof dish with the vegetable mixture. Sprinkle over the grated cheese and top with the haddock fillets. Broil for 10–15 minutes, until cooked. Serve hot, garnished with a lattice of long chives.

Turbot in Parchment

Cooking in parcels is not new, but it is an ideal way to cook fish. Serve this dish plain or with a little hollandaise sauce and let each person open their own parcel to savor the aroma.

INGREDIENTS

Serves 4

2 carrots, cut into thin julienne strips

2 zucchini, cut into thin julienne strips

2 leeks, cut into thin julienne strips

1 fennel bulb, cut into thin julienne strips

2 tomatoes, skinned, seeded and diced

2 tablespoons chopped fresh dill, tarragon or chervil

4 turbot fillets, about 7 ounces each, cut in half

4 teaspoons olive oil

¼ cup white wine or fish stock

salt and freshly ground black pepper

1 Cut 4 pieces of non-stick baking paper, about 18 inches long. Fold each piece in half and cut into a heart shape.

2 Open the paper hearts. Arrange one-quarter of each of the vegetables next to the fold of each heart. Sprinkle with salt and pepper and half the chopped herbs. Arrange 2 pieces of turbot fillet over each bed of vegetables, overlapping the thin end of one piece and the thicker end of the other. Sprinkle the remaining herbs, the olive oil and wine or stock evenly over the fish.

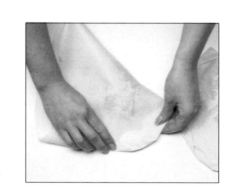

3 Fold the top half of one of the paper hearts over the fish and vegetables and, beginning at the rounded end, fold the edges of the paper over, twisting and folding to form an airtight package. Repeat with the remaining three.

4 Place the parcels onto baking sheets and bake at 375°F for about 10 minutes, or until the paper is lightly browned and puffed up. Slide each parcel onto a warmed serving plate and serve immediately.

Fillets of Hake Baked with Thyme

Quick cooking is the essence of this dish. Use the freshest garlic available and, if there is no fresh thyme, use half the amount of dried thyme.

INGREDIENTS

Serves 4

4 hake fillets, 6 ounces each

1 shallot, finely chopped

2 garlic cloves, thinly sliced

4 fresh thyme sprigs

juice of 1 lemon

2 tablespoons extra virgin olive oil

salt and freshly ground black pepper

finely grated lemon rind and fresh thyme
    sprigs, to garnish

2 Season well with salt and freshly ground pepper.

3 Drizzle on the lemon juice and olive oil. Bake in a preheated oven at 350°F for about 15 minutes or until the fish flakes easily. Serve, garnished with finely grated lemon rind and fresh thyme sprigs.

VARIATIONS

If hake is not available, you can use cod or haddock fillets for this recipe. You can also use a mixture of fresh herbs, such as tarragon, parsley and chervil.

1 Arrange the hake fillets on the base of a large roasting pan. Scatter the shallot, garlic cloves and thyme on top.

COOK'S TIP

Hake is a round fish found extensively in the North and South Atlantic oceans and is extremely popular in Spain and Portugal. Its milky white flesh is delicate in flavor and quite fragile, so fillets need very careful handling, as they break up easily.

Fish Steaks with Mustard Sauce

This mustard sauce turns a plain fish into something special.

INGREDIENTS

Serves 4-6

4–6 halibut or turbot steaks,
   1 inch thick
4 tablespoons (½ stick) butter, melted
salt and freshly ground black pepper
frisée and lemon wedges, to garnish

For the mustard sauce
¼ cup Dijon mustard
1¼ cups heavy cream
½ teaspoon superfine sugar
1 tablespoon white wine vinegar or
   lemon juice

1 Season the fish steaks with salt and pepper. Arrange them on an oiled rack in a broiler pan and brush the tops of the steaks with melted butter.

2 Broil about 4 inches from the heat, for 4–5 minutes on each side, or until cooked through. Brush with more melted butter when you turn the steaks.

3 Meanwhile, make the sauce. Combine the ingredients in a saucepan and bring to a boil, whisking constantly. Simmer, whisking, until the sauce thickens. Remove from the heat, set aside and keep warm.

4 Transfer the fish to warmed plates. Spoon on the sauce and serve immediately, garnished with frisée and lemon wedges.

Sea Bream with Orange Sauce

Sea bream is a taste revelation to anyone not yet familiar with its creamy rich flavor. The fish has a firm white flesh that goes perfectly with a rich butter sauce, sharpened here with a dash of frozen orange juice concentrate.

INGREDIENTS

Serves 2

2 sea bream (12 ounces each), scaled
    and gutted

2 teaspoons Dijon mustard

1 teaspoon fennel seeds

2 tablespoons olive oil

1 small bunch watercress

6 ounces mixed salad greens, such as oak
    leaf lettuce or frisée

baked potatoes and orange slices, to serve

For the sauce

2 tablespoons frozen orange
    juice concentrate

12 tablespoons unsalted butter, diced

salt and cayenne pepper

1 Slash the bream diagonally four times on either side with a sharp knife. Combine the mustard and fennel seeds, then spread over both sides of the fish. Moisten with oil and broil for 12 minutes, turning once.

2 Place the orange juice concentrate in a bowl and heat over 1 inch of boiling water. Remove the pan from the heat and gradually whisk the butter into the juice until creamy. Season, cover and set aside.

3 Moisten the watercress and salad greens with the remaining olive oil. Arrange the fish on two large plates, spoon the sauce over them and serve with the salad greens, baked potatoes and orange slices.

COOK'S TIP

For speedy baked potatoes, microwave small potatoes on 100% high power for 8 minutes, then crisp in an oven preheated to 400°F for another 10 minutes. Split, insert butter and serve.

Mackerel with Mustard and Lemon Butter

Look for bright, firm-looking, really fresh mackerel.

Serves 4

4 fresh mackerel, about 10 ounces each, gutted and cleaned

1 bunch baby spinach

For the mustard and lemon butter

8 tablespoons (1 stick) butter, melted

2 tablespoons whole-grain mustard

grated rind of 1 lemon

2 tablespoons lemon juice

3 tablespoons chopped fresh parsley

salt and freshly ground black pepper

1 To prepare each mackerel, cut off the heads just behind the gills, using a sharp knife, then cut along the belly so that the fish can be opened out flat.

2 Place the fish on a board, skin side up, and, with the heel of your hand, press along the backbone to loosen it.

3 Turn the fish the right way up and pull the bone away from the flesh. Remove the tail and cut each fish in half lengthwise. Wash and pat dry.

4 Score the skin three or four times, then season the fish. To make the mustard and lemon butter, combine the melted butter, mustard, lemon rind and juice, parsley and seasoning. Place the mackerel on a broiler pan. Brush a little of the butter on the mackerel and broil for 5 minutes on each side, basting occasionally, until cooked through.

5 Arrange the spinach leaves in the center of 4 large plates. Place the mackerel on top. Heat the remaining butter in a small pan until sizzling and pour it over the mackerel. Serve immediately.

Tuna and Corn Fish Cakes

These economical little tuna fish cakes are quick to make. Use fresh mashed potatoes or make a quick version with instant mashed potatoes.

INGREDIENTS

Serves 4

2 cups cooked mashed potatoes

1 can (7 ounces) tuna fish in soy oil, drained and flaked

¾ cup canned corn

2 tablespoons chopped fresh parsley

½ cup fresh white or brown bread crumbs

salt and freshly ground black pepper

lemon wedges, to garnish

fresh vegetables, to serve

1 Place the mashed potatoes in a bowl and stir in the tuna fish, corn and chopped parsley.

2 Season to taste with salt and pepper, then shape into 8 patty shapes with your hands.

3 Spread out the bread crumbs on a plate and gently press the fish cakes into the bread crumbs to coat lightly, then transfer to a baking sheet.

4 Cook the fish cakes under a moderately hot broiler until crisp and golden brown, turning once. Serve hot with the lemon wedges and fresh vegetables.

COOK'S TIP

For simple variations, which are just as nutritious, try using canned sardines, red or pink salmon, or smoked mackerel in place of the tuna fish.

Trout with Almonds

This simple and quick recipe doubles easily—you can cook the trout in two frying pans or in batches. In Normandy, hazelnuts might be used in place of almonds.

INGREDIENTS

Serves 2

2 trout, about 12 ounces each, cleaned

¾ cup plain flour

4 tablespoons (½ stick) butter

¼ cup sliced almonds

2 tablespoons dry white wine

salt and freshly ground black pepper

1 Rinse the trout and pat dry. Put the flour in a large plastic bag and season with salt and pepper. Place the trout, 1 at a time, in the bag and shake to coat with flour. Shake off the excess and discard the remaining flour.

2 Melt half the butter in a large frying pan over medium heat. When it is foamy, add the trout and cook for 6–7 minutes on each side, until golden brown and the flesh next to the bone is opaque. Transfer the fish to warmed plates and keep warm.

3 Add the remaining butter to the pan and cook the almonds until just lightly browned. Add the wine to the pan and bring to a boil. Boil for 1 minute, stirring constantly, until slightly syrupy. Pour or spoon the sauce over the fish and serve immediately.

St. Rémy Tuna

St. Rémy is a beautiful village in Provence in the south of France. Herbs, such as thyme, rosemary and oregano, grow wild on the nearby hillside and feature in many of the recipes from this area.

INGREDIENTS

Serves 4

4 tuna steaks, about 6–7 ounces each, 1 inch thick

2–3 tablespoons olive oil

3–4 garlic cloves, finely chopped

¼ cup dry white wine

3 ripe plum tomatoes, skinned, seeded and chopped

1 teaspoon dried **herbes de Provence**

salt and freshly ground black pepper

fresh basil leaves, to garnish

fried potatoes, to serve

1 Season the tuna steaks with salt and pepper. Set a heavy frying pan over high heat until very hot, add the oil and swirl to coat. Add the tuna steaks and press down gently, then reduce the heat to medium and cook for 6–8 minutes, turning once, until just slightly pink in the center.

2 Transfer the steaks to a serving plate and cover to keep warm.

3 Add the garlic to the pan and fry for 15–20 seconds, stirring constantly, then pour in the wine and boil until it is reduced by half. Add the tomatoes and dried herbs and cook for 2–3 minutes, until bubbling. Season with pepper and pour the sauce over the fish steaks. Garnish with fresh basil leaves and serve with fried potatoes.

COOK'S TIP

Tuna is often served pink in the middle, rather like beef. If you prefer it cooked through, reduce the heat and cook for an extra few minutes.

Fillets of Pink Trout with Tarragon Sauce

Trout fillets are increasingly available from supermarkets. Otherwise, buy four whole trout and ask your fish store to fillet and skin them for you.

INGREDIENTS

Serves 4

2 tablespoons butter

8 trout fillets

salt and freshly ground black pepper

new potatoes and runner beans, to serve

For the tarragon sauce

2 large scallions, white parts
  only, chopped

½ cucumber, peeled, seeded, and cut into
  short batons

1 teaspoon cornstarch

⅔ cup light cream

¼ cup dry sherry

2 tablespoons chopped fresh tarragon

1 tomato, seeded and chopped

1 Melt the butter in a large skillet. Season the trout fillets with salt and pepper and cook for about 6 minutes, turning once. Transfer the fillets to a plate, cover, and keep warm.

2 To make the sauce, add the scallions and cucumber batons to the same skillet and sauté over a low heat, stirring constantly, until they are soft, but not colored.

3 Remove the skillet from the heat and stir in the cornstarch.

4 Return the skillet to the heat and pour in the light cream and sherry. Simmer, stirring constantly, until thickened.

5 Add the chopped tarragon and tomato and season to taste.

6 Transfer the trout fillets to 4 individual serving plates and spoon the sauce over them. Serve immediately with buttered new potatoes and runner beans.

Trout Wrapped in a Blanket

The "blanket" of bacon bastes the fish during cooking, keeping it moist and adding flavor at the same time.

INGREDIENTS

Serves 4

juice of ½ lemon

4 trout, about 10 ounces each

4 thyme sprigs

8 slices bacon

salt and freshly ground black pepper

chopped fresh parsley and thyme sprigs,
    to garnish

lemon wedges, to serve

1 Squeeze lemon juice over the skin and in the cavity of each fish, season all over, then put a thyme sprig in each cavity.

2 Stretch each bacon slice using the back of a knife, then wind 2 slices around each fish. Preheat the oven to 400°F.

3 Place the fish in a lightly greased shallow baking dish with the loose ends of bacon tucked underneath to prevent them from unwinding.

4 Bake for 15–20 minutes, until the trout flesh flakes easily when tested with the point of a sharp knife and the bacon is crisp and is just beginning to brown.

5 To serve, sprinkle the trout with chopped parsley, then garnish with sprigs of thyme and accompany with lemon wedges.

COOK'S TIP

You can partially prepare this dish in advance. The trout can be wrapped in bacon and kept covered in the refrigerator until you are ready to cook. Return them to room temperature about 20 minutes before baking.

Salmon with Watercress Sauce

Adding the watercress right at the end of cooking lets it retain much of its flavor and color.

INGREDIENTS

Serves 4

1¼ cups crème fraîche

2 tablespoons chopped fresh tarragon

2 tablespoons unsalted butter

1 tablespoon sunflower oil

4 salmon fillets, skinned and boned

1 garlic clove, crushed

scant ½ cup dry white wine

1 bunch watercress

salt and freshly ground black pepper

salad greens, to serve

1 Gently heat the crème fraîche in a small pan until just beginning to boil. Remove the pan from the heat and stir in half the tarragon. Let the herb cream infuse while you cook the fish.

2 Heat the butter and oil in a frying pan, add the salmon and fry for 3–5 minutes on each side. Remove from the pan and keep warm.

3 Add the garlic to the pan and fry for 1 minute, then pour in the wine and let it bubble until reduced to about 1 tablespoon.

4 Meanwhile, strip the leaves off the watercress stalks and chop finely. Discard any damaged leaves. (Save the watercress stalks for soup, if desired.)

5 Strain the herb cream into the pan and cook for a few minutes, stirring until the sauce has thickened. Stir in the remaining chopped tarragon and the watercress, then cook for a few minutes, until wilted but still bright green. Season and serve immediately, spooned over the salmon. Serve with salad greens.

Salmon with Green Peppercorns

A fashionable discovery of nouvelle cuisine, green peppercorns add piquancy to all kinds of sauces and stews. Available pickled in jars or cans, they are great to keep on hand in your pantry.

INGREDIENTS

Serves 4

1 tablespoon butter

2 or 3 shallots, finely chopped

1 tablespoon brandy (optional)

¼ cup white wine

6 tablespoons fish or chicken stock

½ cup heavy cream

2–3 tablespoons green peppercorns in brine, rinsed

1–2 tablespoons vegetable oil

4 pieces salmon fillet, 6–7 ounces each

salt and freshly ground black pepper

fresh parsley, to garnish

1 Melt the butter in a heavy saucepan over medium heat. Add the shallots and cook for 1–2 minutes, until just softened but not colored.

2 Add the brandy, if using, and the white wine, then add the stock and bring to a boil. Boil vigorously to reduce by three-quarters, stirring occasionally.

3 Reduce the heat, then add the cream and half the pepper-corns, crushing them slightly with the back of a spoon. Cook very gently for 4–5 minutes, until the sauce is slightly thickened, then strain and stir in the remaining peppercorns. Keep the sauce warm over very low heat, stirring occasionally, while you cook the salmon fillets.

4 In a large heavy frying pan, heat the oil over medium-high heat until very hot. Lightly season the salmon and cook for 3–4 minutes, until the flesh is opaque throughout. To check, pierce the fish with the tip of a sharp knife; the juices should run clear. Arrange the fish on warmed plates and pour on the sauce. Garnish with parsley and serve.

Salmon with Tarragon Mushroom Sauce

Tarragon has a distinctive aniseed flavor that is good with fish, cream and mushrooms. This recipe uses oyster mushrooms to provide both texture and flavor.

INGREDIENTS

Serves 4

4 tablespoons (½ stick) unsalted butter

4 salmon steaks, 6 ounces each

1 shallot, finely chopped

6 ounces assorted wild and cultivated
    mushrooms, such as oyster
    mushrooms, trimmed and sliced

scant 1 cup chicken or vegetable stock

2 teaspoons cornstarch

½ teaspoon mustard

¼ cup crème fraîche

3 tablespoons chopped fresh tarragon

1 teaspoon white wine vinegar

salt and cayenne pepper

boiled new potatoes and green salad,
    to serve

1 Melt half the butter in a large frying pan, season the salmon and cook over medium heat for 8 minutes, turning once. Transfer to a plate, cover and keep warm.

2 Heat the remaining butter in the pan and gently fry the shallot to soften. Add the mushrooms and cook until the juices begin to flow. Add the stock and simmer for 2–3 minutes.

3 Combine the cornstarch and mustard and blend with 1 tablespoon of water. Stir into the mushroom mixture and bring to a simmer, stirring, to thicken. Add the crème fraîche, tarragon, vinegar and salt and pepper to taste.

4 Spoon the mushrooms and sauce over each salmon steak and serve with new potatoes and a green salad.

COOK'S TIP

Fresh tarragon will bruise and darken quickly after chopping, so prepare the herb just before you need it.

Chinese-spiced Fish Fillets

*East meets West with this novel twist
on a classic English dish.*

INGREDIENTS

Serves 4

¾ cup flour

1 teaspoon Chinese five-spice powder

8 skinned fillets of fish, such as plaice or
  lemon sole, about 1¾ pounds total

1 egg, beaten to mix

½ cup fine fresh bread crumbs

peanut oil, for frying

2 tablespoons butter

4 scallions, cut diagonally into thin slices

2 large tomatoes, seeded and diced

2 tablespoons soy sauce

salt and freshly ground black pepper

chives and strips of red bell pepper, to
  garnish

1 Sift the flour together with the
Chinese five-spice powder and
salt and pepper to taste onto a
plate. Dip the fish fillets first in the
seasoned flour, then in beaten egg
and finally in bread crumbs.

2 Pour the oil into a large frying
pan to a depth of ½ inch. Heat
until it is very hot and starting to
sizzle. Add the coated fillets, a few
at a time, and fry for 2–3 minutes,
according to the thickness of the
fillets, until just cooked and golden
brown on both sides. Do not
crowd the pan or the temperature
of the oil will drop and the fish will
absorb too much oil.

3 Drain the fillets on paper
towels, then transfer to plates
and keep warm. Pour off all the oil
from the frying pan and wipe it
out with paper towels.

4 Melt the butter in the pan and
add the scallions and
tomatoes. Stir-fry for 1 minute.
Stir in the soy sauce.

5 Spoon the tomato mixture
over the fish and serve
immediately, garnished with the
chives and pepper strips.

Sole, Spinach and Mushroom Muffins

English muffins, frozen spinach, and a few mushrooms form the basis of this attractive and delicious recipe. Any flat fish may be used, but sole works best of all.

INGREDIENTS

Serves 2

½ cup butter, plus extra for spreading

1 medium onion, chopped

⅔ cup sliced crimini mushrooms

2 fresh thyme sprigs, chopped

10 ounces frozen leaf spinach, thawed

1½ pounds sole fillets, skinned

2 English muffins, split

4 tablespoons crème fraîche

salt and freshly ground black pepper

1 Heat 4 tablespoons of the butter in a pan. Add the onion and sauté over a low heat until it is soft, but not colored.

2 Add the mushrooms and thyme, cover, and cook for a further 2–3 minutes. Remove the lid and increase the heat to drive off excess moisture.

3 Using the back of a large spoon, press the thawed spinach in a strainer to extract all the moisture.

4 Melt 2 tablespoons of the remaining butter in a saucepan. Add the spinach and heat through. Season to taste.

5 Melt the remaining butter in a large skillet. Season the fish with salt and pepper and sauté for 2 minutes on each side.

6 Meanwhile, lightly toast then butter the split English muffins. Divide the fish fillets between the muffin halves, top each with spinach and a layer of mushrooms, then finish with a spoonful of crème fraîche. Sprinkle with a little pepper and serve immediately.

Smoked Haddock and Pasta in Parsley Sauce

*A creamy and delicious pasta dish
with a crunchy almond topping.*

INGREDIENTS

Serves 4

1 pound smoked haddock fillet

1 small leek or onion, sliced thickly

1¼ cups milk

1 bouquet garni (bay leaf, thyme and
    parsley stalks)

2 tablespoons margarine

2 tablespoons flour

8 ounces pasta shells

2 tablespoons chopped fresh parsley

salt and freshly ground black pepper

½ cup toasted sliced almonds, to garnish

3 Put the margarine, flour and
reserved milk into a pan. Bring
to a boil and whisk constantly until
smooth. Season, then add the fish
and leek.

4 Cook the pasta in a large pan
of boiling water until tender,
but still firm to the bite. Drain and
stir into the sauce with the chopped
parsley. Serve immediately,
scattered with almonds.

1 Remove all the skin and any
bones from the haddock. Put
into a pan with the leek, milk and
bouquet garni. Bring to a boil,
cover and simmer gently for 8–10
minutes, until the fish flakes easily.

2 Strain, reserving the milk for
making the sauce, and discard
the bouquet garni.

Pan-fried Garlic Sardines

Lightly fry a sliced clove of garlic to garnish the fish. This dish could also be made with fresh anchovies, if available.

INGREDIENTS

Serves 4

2½ pounds fresh sardines

2 tablespoons olive oil

4 garlic cloves

finely grated rind of 2 lemons

2 tablespoons chopped fresh parsley

salt and freshly ground black pepper

For the tomato bread

2 large ripe beefsteak tomatoes

8 slices crusty bread, toasted

1 Gut and clean the sardines thoroughly.

2 Heat the oil in a frying pan and add the garlic cloves. Cook until soft.

3 Add the sardines and fry for 4–5 minutes. Sprinkle on the lemon rind, parsley and seasoning.

4 Cut the tomatoes in half and rub them onto the toast, discarding the skins. Serve the sardines with the tomato toast.

Red Snapper with Cilantro Salsa

Snapper is a firm fish with little fat and benefits from a sauce with lots of texture and flavor.

Serves 4

4 red snapper fillets, about 6 ounces each

1½ tablespoons vegetable oil

1 tablespoon butter

salt and freshly ground black pepper

For the salsa

1 bunch fresh cilantro, stalks removed

1 cup olive oil

2 garlic cloves, chopped

2 tomatoes, seeded and chopped

2 tablespoons fresh orange juice

1 tablespoon sherry vinegar

cilantro sprigs and orange peel, to garnish

salad, to serve (optional)

3 Rinse the fish fillets and pat dry, then sprinkle with salt and pepper on both sides. Heat the oil and butter in a large frying pan. When hot, add the fish and cook for 2–3 minutes on each side or until opaque throughout. Cook the fish in two batches, if necessary.

4 Transfer the fillets to warmed serving plates. Top with a spoonful of salsa. Serve, garnished with cilantro and orange peel and with a salad, if desired.

1 To make the salsa, place the cilantro, oil and garlic in a food processor or blender. Process until almost smooth. Add the tomatoes and pulse on and off several times; the mixture should be slightly chunky.

2 Transfer the mixture to a bowl. Stir in the orange juice, vinegar and salt to taste, then set the salsa aside.

Spaghettini with Vodka and Caviar

This is an elegant, yet easy, way to serve spaghettini. In Rome it is an after-theater favorite.

Serves 4

¼ cup olive oil

3 scallions, thinly sliced

1 garlic clove, finely chopped

½ cup vodka

⅓ cup heavy cream

⅔ cup black or red caviar

1 pound spaghettini

salt and freshly ground black pepper

COOK'S TIP

The finest caviar is salted sturgeon roe. Red "caviar" is dog salmon roe, cheaper and often saltier than sturgeon roe.

1 Heat the oil in a small frying pan. Add the scallions and garlic, and cook gently for 4–5 minutes, until softened.

2 Add the vodka and cream, and cook over low heat for about 5–8 more minutes.

3 Remove from the heat and stir in the caviar. Season with salt and pepper, as necessary.

4 Meanwhile, cook the pasta in a large pan of rapidly boiling salted water until tender, but still firm to the bite. Drain the pasta, and toss immediately to coat with the sauce. Serve immediately.

Penne with Tuna and Mozzarella

This tasty sauce is quickly made from ingredients you are likely to have on hand, with the simple addition of fresh mozzarella and parsley. If possible, use tuna canned in olive oil.

Serves 4

14 ounces penne, or other short pasta

1 tablespoon capers, in brine or salt

2 garlic cloves

3 tablespoons chopped fresh parsley

1 can (7 ounces) of tuna, drained

5 tablespoons olive oil

4 ounces mozzarella cheese, cut into small dice

salt and freshly ground black pepper

1 Bring a pan of salted water to the boil and cook the pasta according to package instructions.

2 Rinse the capers well in water. Chop them finely with the garlic. Combine with the parsley and the tuna. Stir in the oil, and season to taste.

3 Drain the pasta when it is just tender, but still firm to the bite. Transfer to a large frying pan. Add the tuna sauce and the diced mozzarella. Cook over medium heat, stirring constantly, until the cheese is just beginning to melt. Serve immediately.

Tagliatelle with Smoked Salmon

This is a pretty pasta sauce that tastes as good as it looks. The light texture of the cucumber perfectly complements the fish. Different effects and color combinations can be achieved by using green, white or red tagliatelle—or even a mixture of all three.

INGREDIENTS

Serves 4

12 ounces dried or fresh tagliatelle

½ cucumber

6 tablespoons (¾ stick) butter

grated rind of 1 orange

2 tablespoons chopped fresh dill

1¼ cups light cream or half-and-half

1 tablespoon orange juice

4 ounces smoked salmon, skinned

salt and freshly ground black pepper

1 If using dried pasta, cook in lightly salted boiling water following the manufacturer's instructions on the package. If using fresh pasta, cook in lightly salted boiling water for 2–3 minutes or until just tender but still firm to the bite.

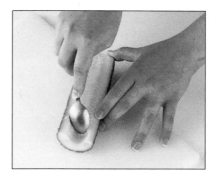

2 Using a sharp knife, cut the cucumber in half lengthwise. Using a small spoon, scoop out the cucumber seeds and discard.

3 Turn the cucumber halves onto their flat sides and slice thinly.

4 Melt the butter in a heavy saucepan, add the grated orange rind and fresh dill and stir well. Add the cucumber and cook gently over low heat for about 2 minutes, stirring occasionally.

5 Add the cream, orange juice and seasoning to taste and simmer gently for 1 minute.

6 Meanwhile, cut the salmon into thin strips.

7 Stir the salmon into the sauce and heat through.

8 Drain the pasta thoroughly and toss it in the sauce. Serve immediately.

COOK'S TIP

A more economical way to make this special-occasion sauce is to use smoked salmon pieces, sold relatively inexpensively at most delicatessens and some supermarkets. (These are just scraps and awkwardly shaped pieces that are unsuitable for recipes requiring whole slices of smoked salmon.) Smoked trout is a less expensive alternative, but it lacks the rich flavor and color of smoked salmon.

Sicilian Spaghetti with Sardines

A traditional dish from Sicily, with ingredients that are common to many parts of the Mediterranean.

INGREDIENTS

Serves 4

12 fresh sardines, cleaned and boned

1 cup olive oil

1 onion, chopped

¼ cup fresh dill, chopped

½ cup pine nuts

½ cup raisins, soaked in water

½ cup fresh bread crumbs

1 pound spaghetti

flour for dusting

salt

1 Wash the sardines and pat them dry with paper towels. Open them out flat, then cut in half lengthwise.

2 Heat 2 tablespoons of the oil in a pan, add the onion and fry until golden. Add the dill and cook gently for 1–2 minutes. Add the pine nuts and raisins and season with salt to taste. Dry-fry the bread crumbs in a frying pan until golden. Set aside.

3 Cook the spaghetti in boiling salted water according to the instructions on the package, until tender, but still firm to the bite. Heat the remaining oil in a pan. Dust the sardines with flour and fry in the hot oil for 2–3 minutes. Drain on paper towels.

4 Drain the spaghetti and return to the pan. Add the onion mixture and toss well to coat. Transfer the spaghetti mixture to a warmed serving platter and arrange the fried sardines on top. Sprinkle with the toasted bread crumbs and serve immediately.

COOK'S TIP

Sardines are actually baby pilchards and weigh about 4 ounces. They are covered in very fine scales that are most easily removed with your hand, rather than with a scaling knife. Hold the fish by the tail under cold running water and rub your thumb and fingers gently along the body down to the head.

Fish Goujons

Flat fish is ideal for making goujons. Serve with this delicious mock tartar sauce quickly made with capers, cornichons, and mayonnaise.

Serves 4

1½ pounds flat fish fillets

1 tablespoon chopped fresh tarragon

3 cups white bread crumbs

2 eggs, lightly beaten

For the sauce

1 tablespoon capers, drained

1 tablespoon cornichons, drained

⅔ cup mayonnaise

salt and freshly ground black pepper

1 Using a sharp knife, cut the fish fillets into strips. Preheat the oven to 425°F and lightly grease a cookie sheet.

2 In a mixing bowl, stir the tarragon and bread crumbs together well.

3 One at a time, dip the fish strips into the egg, then in the bread crumb mixture, coating them thoroughly. Place the fish strips on the cookie sheet and cook in the oven for 10 minutes.

4 Meanwhile, make the sauce. Roughly chop the capers and cornichons and stir into the mayonnaise. Season to taste with salt and pepper and serve with the crispy goujons.

Fusilli with Smoked Trout

The smoked trout and creamy sauce blend beautifully with the still crunchy vegetables.

INGREDIENTS

Serves 4–6

2 carrots, cut into julienne sticks

1 leek, cut into julienne sticks

2 stalks celery, cut into julienne sticks

⅔ cup vegetable stock

8 ounces smoked trout fillets, skinned and cut into strips

8 ounces cream cheese

⅔ cup medium sweet white wine or fish stock

1 tablespoon chopped fresh dill or fennel

8 ounces long curly fusilli

salt and freshly ground black pepper

dill sprigs, to garnish

1 Put the carrots, leek and celery into a pan with the vegetable stock. Bring to a boil and cook quickly for 4–5 minutes, until the vegetables are tender and most of the stock has evaporated. Remove from the heat and add the smoked trout.

2 To make the sauce, put the cream cheese and wine or fish stock into a saucepan, heat and whisk until smooth. Season with salt and pepper. Add the chopped dill.

3 Cook the fusilli in a large pan of boiling salted water, according to the package instructions, until tender, but firm to the bite. Drain thoroughly.

4 Return the fusilli to the pan with the sauce, toss lightly and transfer to a serving bowl. Top with the cooked vegetables and trout. Serve immediately, garnished with dill sprigs.

Farfalle with Smoked Salmon and Dill

This quick, luxurious and quite delicious sauce for pasta has now become very fashionable in Italy.

INGREDIENTS

Serves 4

6 scallions, sliced

4 tablespoons (½ stick) butter

6 tablespoons dry white wine or vermouth

2 cups heavy cream

freshly grated nutmeg

8 ounces smoked salmon

2 tablespoons chopped fresh dill

freshly squeezed lemon juice

1 pound farfalle (pasta bows)

salt and freshly ground black pepper

fresh dill sprigs, to garnish

1 Slice the scallions finely. Melt the butter in a saucepan and fry the scallions for about 1 minute, until softened.

2 Add the wine and boil hard to reduce to about 2 tablespoons. Stir in the cream and add salt, pepper and nutmeg to taste. Bring to a boil and simmer for 2–3 minutes, until slightly thickened.

3 Cut the smoked salmon into 1-inch squares and stir into the sauce, together with the dill. Add a little lemon juice to taste. Keep warm.

4 Cook the pasta in plenty of boiling salted water as directed. Drain well. Toss with the sauce and serve immediately, garnished with sprigs of dill.

SEAFOOD
DISHES

~

Noodles with Tomatoes and Shrimps

Influences from Italy and the East combine in this dish.

INGREDIENTS

Serves 4

12 ounces somen noodles

3 tablespoons olive oil

20 raw jumbo shrimp, peeled and
 deveined

2 garlic cloves, finely chopped

3–4 tablespoons sun-dried tomato paste

salt and freshly ground black pepper

For the garnish

handful of basil leaves

2 tablespoons sun-dried tomatoes in oil,
 drained and cut into strips

1 Cook the noodles in a large saucepan of boiling water until tender, following the directions on the package. Drain well.

2 Heat half the oil in a large frying pan. Add the shrimp and garlic and fry them over medium heat for 3–5 minutes, until the shrimp turn pink and are firm to the touch.

3 Stir in 1 tablespoon of the sun-dried tomato paste and mix well. Using a slotted spoon, transfer the shrimp to a bowl and keep hot.

4 Reheat the oil remaining in the pan. Stir in the rest of the oil with the remaining sun-dried tomato paste. You may need to add a spoonful of water if the mixture is very thick.

5 When the mixture starts to sizzle, toss in the well-drained noodles. Add salt and pepper to taste and mix well.

6 Return the shrimp to the pan and toss well to combine. Serve immediately, garnished with the basil leaves and strips of sun-dried tomatoes.

COOK'S TIP

Ready-made sun-dried tomato paste is widely available. However, you can make your own simply by processing bottled sun-dried tomatoes with their oil. You could also add a couple of anchovy fillets and some capers, if desired.

Shrimp and Fish in an Herb Sauce

Bengalis are famous for their seafood dishes and always use mustard oil in recipes because it imparts a unique flavor and aroma. No feast is complete without one of these celebrated fish dishes.

INGREDIENTS

Serves 4–6

3 garlic cloves

2-inch piece fresh ginger

1 large leek, roughly chopped

4 green chilies

1 teaspoon vegetable oil (optional)

¼ cup mustard oil

1 tablespoon ground coriander

½ teaspoon fennel seeds

1 tablespoon crushed yellow mustard
    seeds or 1 teaspoon mustard powder

¾ cup thick coconut milk

8 ounces monkfish, sliced

8 ounces raw jumbo shrimp, peeled and
    deveined with tails intact

salt

1 bunch fresh cilantro leaves, chopped

green chilies, to garnish

1 In a food processor, grind the garlic, ginger, leek and chilies into a coarse paste. Add vegetable oil if the mixture is too dry.

2 In a frying pan, heat the mustard oil with the paste until it is well blended. Keep the window open and take care not to overheat the mixture, as any smoke from the mustard oil will sting the eyes and irritate the nose.

3 Add the ground coriander, fennel seeds, mustard and coconut milk. Gently bring to a boil, then simmer, uncovered, for about 5 minutes.

4 Add the fish and simmer for 2 minutes, then fold in the shrimp and cook until the shrimp turn a bright orange-pink color. Season with salt, fold in the cilantro leaves and serve hot. Garnish with green chilies.

Sweet-and-sour Shrimp

It is best to use raw shrimp if available. If you are using cooked ones, add them to the sauce without the initial deep-frying.

INGREDIENTS

Serves 4–6

1 pound raw jumbo shrimp in
  their shells
vegetable oil, for deep-frying
lettuce leaves, to serve

For the sauce

1 tablespoon vegetable oil
1 tablespoon finely chopped scallions
2 teaspoons finely chopped fresh
  ginger
2 tablespoons light soy sauce
2 tablespoons light brown sugar
3 tablespoons rice vinegar
1 tablespoon Chinese rice wine or
  dry sherry
about ½ cup chicken or vegetable stock
1 tablespoon cornstarch paste
few drops sesame oil

1 Pull the soft legs off the shrimp without removing the shells. Rinse and dry well with paper towels.

2 Heat the vegetable oil in a large pan or deep-fryer to 350°F and deep-fry the shrimp for 35–40 seconds or until their color changes from gray to bright orange. Remove and drain on paper towels.

3 To make the sauce, heat the oil in a preheated wok, add the scallions and ginger, followed by the seasonings and stock, and bring to a boil.

4 Add the shrimp to the sauce, blend well, then thicken the sauce with the cornstarch paste, stirring until smooth. Sprinkle with the sesame oil. Serve on a bed of lettuce.

Green Shrimp Curry

A popular, fragrant, creamy curry that takes very little time to prepare. It can also be made with thin strips of chicken meat.

INGREDIENTS

Serves 4–6

2 tablespoons vegetable oil

2 tablespoons green curry paste

1 pound raw jumbo shrimp, peeled
   and deveined

4 kaffir lime leaves, torn

1 lemon grass stalk, bruised and chopped

1 cup coconut milk

2 tablespoons fish sauce

½ cucumber, seeded and cut into
   thin batons

10–15 basil leaves

4 green chilies, sliced, to garnish

1 Heat the oil in a frying pan. Add the green curry paste and fry until bubbling and fragrant.

2 Add the shrimp, kaffir lime leaves and lemon grass. Fry for 1–2 minutes, until the shrimp have just turned pink.

3 Stir in the coconut milk and bring to a gentle boil. Simmer, stirring occasionally, for about 5 minutes or until the shrimp are tender. Do not overcook them.

4 Stir in the fish sauce, cucumber and basil, then top with the green chilies and serve.

Crumb-coated Shrimp

Serve these crunchy breaded shrimp with a homemade or store-bought dipping sauce of your choice.

INGREDIENTS

Serves 4

1½ cups polenta

about 1–2 teaspoons cayenne pepper

½ teaspoon ground cumin

1 teaspoon salt

2 tablespoons chopped fresh cilantro
   or parsley

2¼ pounds large raw shrimp, peeled
   and deveined

flour, for dredging

¼ cup vegetable oil

4 ounces coarsely grated Cheddar cheese

lime wedges and tomato salsa or relish,
   to serve

1 Mix the polenta, cayenne pepper, cumin, salt and cilantro in a bowl.

2 Coat the shrimp lightly in flour, then dip them in water and roll in the polenta mixture to coat evenly.

3 Heat the oil in a frying pan. When hot, add the shrimp, in batches if necessary. Cook for 2–3 minutes on each side, until they are cooked through. Drain on paper towels.

4 Preheat the broiler. Place the shrimp in a baking dish or in 4 individual flameproof dishes. Sprinkle on the cheese. Bake for 2–3 minutes. Serve with lime wedges and tomato salsa or relish.

Shrimp Curry with Quails' Eggs

Quails' eggs are available at specialty stores and delicatessens. Hens' eggs may be substituted if quails' eggs are hard to find. Use 1 hen's egg to every 4 quails' eggs.

INGREDIENTS

Serves 4

12 quails' eggs

2 tablespoons vegetable oil

4 shallots or 1 medium onion, finely chopped

1-inch piece fresh ginger, finely chopped

2 garlic cloves, crushed

2-inch piece lemon grass, finely shredded

1–2 small, fresh red chilies, seeded and finely chopped

½ teaspoon turmeric

½-inch-square piece shrimp paste or 1 tablespoon fish sauce

2 pounds raw shrimp, peeled and deveined

1⅔ cups canned coconut milk

1¼ cups chicken stock

4 ounces spinach, roughly shredded

2 teaspoons sugar

½ teaspoon salt

2 scallions, green part only, shredded, and 2 tablespoons dry shredded coconut, to garnish

1 Cook the quails' eggs in boiling water for 8 minutes. Refresh in cold water, peel and then set aside.

2 Heat the vegetable oil in a large wok, add the shallots, ginger and garlic and soften without coloring. Add the lemon grass, chilies, turmeric and shrimp paste and fry briefly to bring out their flavors.

3 Add the shrimp and fry briefly. Pour the coconut milk through a strainer over a bowl, then add the thin part of the milk with the chicken stock. Add the spinach, sugar and salt and bring to the boil. Simmer for 6–8 minutes.

4 Transfer to a serving dish, halve the quails' eggs and toss in the sauce. Scatter with the scallions and the shredded coconut and serve.

Indonesian Pork and Shrimp Rice

Nasi Goreng is an attractive way of using up leftovers and appears in many variations throughout Indonesia. Rice is the main ingredient, although almost anything can be added for color and flavor.

INGREDIENTS

Serves 4–6

3 eggs

¼ cup vegetable oil

6 shallots, or 1 large onion, chopped

2 garlic cloves, crushed

1-inch piece fresh ginger, chopped

2–3 small red chilies, seeded and
    finely chopped

1 tablespoon tamarind sauce

½-inch square piece shrimp paste or
    1 tablespoon fish sauce

½ teaspoon turmeric

2 tablespoons unsweetened cream of
    coconut

juice of 2 limes

2 teaspoons sugar

12 ounces lean pork or chicken breasts,
    skinned and sliced

12 ounces raw or cooked shrimp, peeled

1 cup bean sprouts

1 small bunch spinach, shredded

1 cup frozen peas, thawed

8 ounces long grain rice, cooked

salt

1 small bunch cilantro or basil, roughly
    chopped, to garnish

1 In a bowl, beat the eggs with a pinch of salt. Heat a non-stick frying pan over medium heat. Pour in the eggs and move the pan around until they begin to set. When set, roll up, slice thinly, cover and set aside.

2 Heat 1 tablespoon of the oil in a preheated wok and fry the shallots until evenly browned. Remove from the wok, set aside and keep warm.

3 Heat the remaining 3 tablespoons of oil in the wok, add the garlic, ginger and chilies, and soften without coloring. Stir in the tamarind and shrimp paste or fish sauce, turmeric, cream of coconut, lime juice, sugar and salt to taste. Cook briefly over medium heat, stirring constantly. Add the pork or chicken and shrimp and fry for 3–4 minutes.

4 Toss the bean sprouts, spinach and peas in the spice mixture and cook briefly. Add the rice and stir-fry for 6–8 minutes, stirring to prevent it from burning. Transfer to a large serving plate, decorate with shredded egg pancake, the fried shallots, and chopped cilantro or basil.

Steamed Chili Mussels

You can add extra red chilies if you really enjoy spicy food.

Serves 6

2 fresh red chilies

6 ripe tomatoes

2 tablespoons peanut oil

2 garlic cloves, crushed

2 shallots, finely chopped

2½ pounds fresh mussels

2 tablespoons white wine

2 tablespoons chopped fresh parsley,
    to garnish

French bread, to serve

1 Seed and roughly chop the fresh chilies. Roughly chop the tomatoes.

2 Heat the oil in a large, heavy-based saucepan and sauté the garlic and shallots over a low heat until soft and translucent.

3 Stir in the chilies and tomatoes and simmer for 10 minutes.

4 Meanwhile, debeard and scrub the mussels. Discard any that do not close when sharply tapped with the back of a knife.

5 Add the mussels and wine to the pan, cover, and cook for 5 minutes, until the mussels have opened. Discard any that remain closed. Scatter over the parsley and serve with French bread.

Spicy Squid

This aromatically spiced squid dish, Cumi Cumi Smoor, is a favorite in Madura, Indonesia and is simple yet utterly delicious. Gone are the days when cleaning squid was such a chore: Now they can be bought ready-cleaned and are available at fish stores, market stalls or the freezers or fish counters of large supermarkets.

INGREDIENTS

Serves 3–4

1½ pounds squid, cleaned

3 tablespoons peanut oil

1 onion, finely chopped

2 garlic cloves, crushed

1 beefsteak tomato, skinned and chopped

1 tablespoon dark soy sauce

½ teaspoon ground nutmeg

6 cloves

⅔ cup water

juice of ½ lemon or lime

salt and freshly ground black pepper

boiled rice, to serve

1 Cut the squid bodies into ribbons and chop the tentacles. Rinse and drain well.

2 Heat a wok, toss in the squid and stir constantly for 2–3 minutes, by which time the squid will have curled into attractive shapes or firm rings. Lift out and set aside in a warm place.

3 Heat the oil in a clean pan and fry the onion and garlic, until soft and beginning to brown. Add the tomato, soy sauce, nutmeg, cloves, water and lemon or lime juice. Bring to a boil, then reduce the heat and add the squid with seasoning to taste.

4 Cook gently for another 3–5 minutes, stirring occasionally. Take care not to overcook the squid. Serve hot or warm, with boiled rice.

VARIATION

Try using 1 pound cooked peeled large shrimp in this recipe. Add them for the final 1–2 minutes.

Farfalle with Shrimp

Creamy sauces are not invariably the best way to serve fish with pasta. This simple, fresh shrimp sauce allows the distinctive flavor of the fish to be identified.

INGREDIENTS

Serves 4

8 ounces fresh or dried farfalle
   (pasta bows)
12 ounces raw or cooked shrimp
8 tablespoons (1 stick) unsalted butter
2 garlic cloves, crushed
3 tablespoons chopped fresh parsley
salt and freshly ground black pepper

1 Cook fresh pasta in boiling salted water for 2–3 minutes, or until tender but still firm to the bite. Cook dried pasta according to the package instructions. Peel and devein the shrimp.

2 Heat the butter in a large heavy saucepan with the garlic and parsley. Toss in the shrimp and sauté for 8 minutes (for cooked shrimp, 4 minutes will be sufficient).

3 Drain the pasta thoroughly and rinse with boiling water to remove any starch.

4 Stir the pasta into the shrimp mixture. Season with salt and pepper to taste and serve.

Tagliatelle with Saffron Mussels

Mussels in a saffron and cream sauce are served with tagliatelle in this recipe, but you can use any other pasta.

INGREDIENTS

Serves 4

4–4½ pounds mussels

⅔ cup dry white wine

2 shallots, chopped

12 ounces dried tagliatelle

2 tablespoons butter

2 garlic cloves, crushed

1 cup heavy cream

generous pinch of saffron strands, soaked
   in 2 tablespoons hot water

1 egg yolk

salt and freshly ground black pepper

2 tablespoons chopped fresh parsley,
   to garnish

1 Scrub the mussels under cold running water. Remove the beards. Discard any mussels with damaged shells or that do not shut immediately when sharply tapped.

2 Place the mussels in a large pan with the wine and shallots. Cover and cook over high heat, shaking the pan occasionally, for 5–8 minutes, until the mussels have opened. Drain the mussels, reserving the liquid. Discard any that remain closed. Shell all but a few of the mussels and keep warm.

3 Bring the reserved cooking liquid to a boil, then boil vigorously to reduce by about half. Strain through a fine sieve into a bowl to remove any grit.

4 Cook the tagliatelle in a pan of boiling salted water, according to the package instructions, until tender, but still firm to the bite.

5 Melt the butter in a pan and fry the garlic for 1 minute. Add the mussel liquid, cream and saffron. Heat gently, until the sauce thickens slightly. Remove from the heat and stir in the egg yolk, shelled mussels and seasoning.

6 Drain the pasta and transfer to serving bowls. Spoon on the sauce and sprinkle with chopped parsley. Garnish with the mussels in shells and serve immediately.

Linguine with Clams

Toss together this sauce for a real seafood flavor and serve with a light mixed salad. Canned clams make this a speedy sauce for those in a real hurry.

INGREDIENTS

Serves 4

12 ounces linguine (thin noodles)

2 tablespoons butter

2 leeks, thinly sliced

⅔ cup dry white wine

4 tomatoes, skinned, seeded and chopped

pinch of ground turmeric (optional)

1 can (9 ounces) clams, drained

2 tablespoons chopped fresh basil

¼ cup crème fraîche

salt and freshly ground black pepper

1 Cook the pasta following the instructions on the package.

2 Meanwhile, melt the butter in a small saucepan and fry the leeks for about 5 minutes until softened but not colored.

3 Add the wine, tomatoes and turmeric, if using, bring to a boil and boil until reduced by half.

4 Stir in the clams, basil, crème fraîche and seasoning to taste and heat through gently without allowing the sauce to boil.

5 Drain the pasta thoroughly and toss it in the sauce to coat. Serve immediately.

Macaroni with Jumbo Shrimp and Ham

This quick-and-easy recipe is an ideal lunch or supper dish.

INGREDIENTS

Serves 4

12 ounces macaroni

3 tablespoons olive oil

12 raw jumbo shrimp, peeled and deveined

1 garlic clove, chopped

6 ounces smoked ham, diced

⅔ cup red wine

½ small head radicchio, shredded

2 egg yolks, beaten

2 tablespoons chopped fresh flat leaf parsley

⅔ cup heavy cream

salt and freshly ground black pepper

shredded fresh basil, to garnish

1 Cook the pasta following the instructions on the package.

2 Meanwhile, heat the oil in a frying pan and cook the shrimp, garlic and ham for about 5 minutes, stirring occasionally, until the shrimp are tender.

3 Add the wine and radicchio, bring to a boil and boil rapidly until the juices are reduced by about half.

4 Stir in the egg yolks, parsley and cream and bring almost to a boil, stirring constantly, then simmer until the sauce thickens slightly. Season to taste.

5 Drain the pasta thoroughly and toss it in the sauce to coat. Serve immediately, garnished with shredded fresh basil.

COOK'S TIP

Flat leaf parsley has more flavor than the curly variety. Finely chop any leftover parsley and freeze it in a small plastic bag. It is then ready to use for cooking, but not garnishing.

Pasta with Scallops in Green Sauce

The striking colors of this dish make it irresistible.

INGREDIENTS

Serves 4

½ cup low-fat crème fraîche

2 teaspoons whole-grain mustard

2 garlic cloves, crushed

2–3 tablespoons fresh lime juice

¼ cup chopped fresh parsley

2 tablespoons snipped chives

12 ounces black tagliatelle

12 large prepared scallops

¼ cup white wine

⅔ cup fish stock

salt and freshly ground black pepper

lime wedges and parsley sprigs, to garnish

1 To make the green sauce, combine the crème fraîche, mustard, garlic, lime juice, herbs and seasoning in a bowl.

2 Cook the pasta in boiling salted water according to the package instructions. Drain well.

3 Slice the scallops in half, horizontally. Keep any coral whole. Put the wine and fish stock into a saucepan. Heat to simmering point. Add the scallops and cook very gently for 3–4 minutes.

4 Remove the scallops. Boil the wine and stock vigorously to reduce by half and add the green sauce to the pan. Heat gently to warm, replace the scallops and cook for 1 minute. Spoon the sauce over the pasta and garnish with lime wedges and parsley.

Seafood Spaghetti

This pasta sauce provides a truly Mediterranean flavor. Serve with thick slices of fresh Italian bread.

INGREDIENTS

Serves 4

1 tablespoon olive oil

12 ounces dried spaghetti

4 tablespoons butter

1 onion, chopped

1 red bell pepper, seeded and chopped

2 garlic cloves, chopped

1 tablespoon paprika

1 pound fresh mussels

⅔ cup dry white wine

2 tablespoons chopped fresh parsley

8 ounces peeled, cooked shrimp

⅔ cup crème fraîche

salt and freshly ground black pepper

finely chopped fresh flat leaf parsley, to garnish

Italian bread, to serve

1 Bring a large saucepan of lightly salted water to a boil. Add the olive oil and spaghetti. Bring back to a boil, lower the heat, and cook for 8–10 minutes, until the spaghetti is tender, but still firm to the bite.

4 Add the wine to the pan and bring to a boil.

2 Melt the butter in a pan and fry the onion, bell pepper, garlic, and paprika for 5 minutes.

3 Debeard and scrub the mussels. Discard any that do not close immediately when sharply tapped with the back of a knife.

5 Stir in the mussels, parsley, and shrimp, cover, and simmer for about 5 minutes, until the mussels have opened. Discard any that remain closed.

6 Remove the shellfish from the pan with a slotted spoon and keep warm. Bring the cooking juices back to a boil and boil rapidly until reduced by half.

7 Stir in the crème fraîche and blend thoroughly. Return the shellfish to the pan and simmer over a low heat for 1 minute to heat through. Taste and season.

8 Drain the spaghetti thoroughly and divide it between individual serving plates. Spoon the shellfish and sauce over the top and toss, using two forks. Garnish with the chopped flat leaf parsley and serve immediately with the Italian bread.

SALADS

~

Warm Fish Salad with Mango Dressing

This salad is best served during the summer months, preferably out-of-doors. The dressing combines the flavor of rich mango with hot chili, ginger and lime.

INGREDIENTS

Serves 4

1 loaf of French bread

4 black bream or porgy, each weighing about 10 ounces

1 tablespoon vegetable oil

1 mango

½-inch piece fresh ginger

1 fresh red chili, seeded and finely chopped

2 tablespoons lime juice

2 tablespoons chopped fresh cilantro

6 ounces young spinach

5 ounces bok choy

6 ounces cherry tomatoes, halved

1 Cut the French loaf into 8-inch lengths. Slice length-ways, then cut into thick fingers. Place the bread on a baking sheet and dry in a preheated oven at 350°F for 15 minutes. Slash the fish deeply on both sides with a sharp knife and moisten with oil. Cook under a preheated broiler or on a barbecue for 6 minutes, turning once.

2 Peel and pit the mango. Slice the flesh and place half of it in a food processor. Peel and finely grate the ginger, then add to the food processor with the chili, lime juice and cilantro. Process until smooth. Adjust to a pouring consistency with 2–3 tablespoons water.

3 Wash the salad greens and spin dry, then divide them equally between 4 serving plates. Place the fish on the leaves. Spoon on the mango dressing and finish with slices of mango and cherry tomato halves. Serve with the fingers of crispy French bread.

COOK'S TIP

Other fish suitable for this salad include salmon, monkfish, tuna, sea bass and halibut. Use fillets, cutlets or steaks.

Spinach Salad with Bacon and Shrimp

Serve this hot salad with plenty of crusty bread for mopping up the delicious juices.

INGREDIENTS

Serves 4

7 tablespoons olive oil

2 tablespoons sherry vinegar

2 garlic cloves, finely chopped

1 teaspoon Dijon mustard

12 cooked jumbo shrimp

4 strips bacon

about 4 ounces fresh young
   spinach leaves

½ head oak leaf lettuce, roughly torn

salt and freshly ground black pepper

1 To make the dressing, whisk together 6 tablespoons of the olive oil with the vinegar, garlic, mustard and seasoning in a small pan. Heat gently until thickened slightly, then keep warm.

2 Carefully peel the shrimp, leaving the tails intact. Set aside.

3 Heat the remaining oil in a frying pan and fry the bacon until golden and crisp, stirring occasionally. Add the shrimp and stir-fry for a few minutes, until warmed through.

4 While the bacon and shrimp are cooking, arrange the spinach and torn oak leaf lettuce leaves on four individual serving plates.

5 Spoon the bacon and shrimp onto the leaves, then pour on the hot dressing. Serve immediately.

COOK'S TIP

Sherry vinegar lends its pungent flavor to this delicious salad. You can buy it at most large supermarkets and delicatessens.

Salmon and Tuna Parcels

You will need fairly large smoked salmon slices as they are wrapped around a light tuna mixture before being served on a vibrant salad.

INGREDIENTS

Serves 4

2 tablespoons low-fat plain yogurt

1 tablespoon sun-dried tomato paste

1 teaspoon whole-grain honey mustard

grated rind and juice of 1 lime

1 can (7 ounces) tuna in brine, drained

5 ounces smoked salmon slices

salt and freshly ground black pepper

fresh mint leaves, to garnish

For the salad

3 tomatoes, sliced

2 kiwi fruit, peeled and sliced

¼ cucumber, cut into julienne sticks

For the mint vinaigrette

1 tablespoon wine vinegar

3 tablespoons olive oil

1 tablespoon chopped fresh mint

COOK'S TIP

Although healthy eating guidelines recommend reducing the amount of fat, particularly saturated fat, in the diet, salad dressings made with polyunsaturated or monounsaturated oil, such as olive oil, can and should be included, in sensible moderation. This recipe is not high in calories, but if weight control is a real issue, use an oil-free dressing instead of vinaigrette.

1 Mix the yogurt, tomato paste and mustard in a bowl. Stir in the grated lime rind and juice. Add the tuna, with black pepper to taste, and mix well.

2 Spread out the salmon slices on a board and spoon some of the tuna mixture onto each piece.

3 Roll up or fold the smoked salmon into neat parcels. Carefully press the edges together to seal.

4 Make the salad. Arrange the tomato and kiwi slices on 4 serving plates. Scatter on the cucumber sticks.

5 Make the vinaigrette. Put all the ingredients in a screw-top jar, season with salt and pepper and shake vigorously. Spoon a little vinaigrette over each salad.

6 Arrange 3–4 salmon parcels on each salad, garnish with the mint leaves and serve.

Warm Salmon Salad

Light and fresh, this salad is perfect for an al fresco summer lunch. Serve it immediately, or you'll find the salad greens will lose their bright color and texture.

INGREDIENTS

Serves 4

1 pound salmon fillet, skinned

2 tablespoons sesame oil

grated rind of ½ orange

juice of 1 orange

1 teaspoon Dijon mustard

1 tablespoon chopped fresh tarragon

3 tablespoons peanut oil

1 cup fine green beans, trimmed

2 ounces mixed salad greens, such as
    young spinach leaves, radicchio, frisée
    and oak leaf lettuce

1 tablespoon toasted sesame seeds

salt and freshly ground black pepper

1 Cut the salmon into bite-size pieces, then make the dressing. Combine the sesame oil, orange rind and juice, mustard, chopped tarragon and seasoning in a bowl. Set aside.

2 Heat the peanut oil in a frying pan. Add the salmon pieces and fry for 3–4 minutes, until lightly browned but still tender inside.

3 Meanwhile, blanch the green beans in boiling salted water for about 5–6 minutes, until they are tender, but still crisp.

4 Add the dressing to the salmon, toss together gently and cook for 30 seconds. Remove the pan from the heat.

5 Arrange the salad greens on 4 serving plates. Drain the beans and toss over the leaves. Spoon over the salmon and cooking juices and serve immediately, sprinkled with the toasted sesame seeds.

Melon and Crab Salad

A perfect summer salad when crab and melon are in generous supply.

INGREDIENTS

Serves 6

1 pound fresh cooked crab meat

½ cup mayonnaise

3 tablespoons sour cream or
   plain yogurt

2 tablespoons olive oil

2 tablespoons fresh lemon or lime juice

2–3 scallions, finely chopped

2 tablespoons finely chopped
   fresh cilantro

¼ teaspoon cayenne pepper

1½ cantaloupe or small honeydew melons

3 medium endives

salt and freshly ground black pepper

fresh cilantro sprigs, to garnish

1 Pick over the crab meat very carefully, removing any bits of shell or cartilage. Leave the pieces of crab meat as large as possible.

2 In a medium-size bowl, combine mayonnaise, sour cream or yogurt, olive oil, lemon or lime juice, scallions, chopped cilantro and cayenne pepper and season to taste with salt and pepper. Mix well, then fold the crab meat into this dressing.

3 Halve the melons and remove and discard the seeds. Cut the melons into thin slices, then remove the rind.

4 Divide the salad between 6 individual serving plates, making a decorative design with the melon slices and whole endive leaves. Place a mound of dressed crab meat on each plate and garnish the salads with one or two fresh cilantro sprigs.

Mediterranean Salad with Basil

A type of Salade Niçoise with pasta, this conjures up all the sunny flavors of the Mediterranean.

INGREDIENTS

Serves 4

8 ounces chunky pasta shapes

1 cup green beans

2 large ripe tomatoes

2 ounces fresh basil leaves

1 can (7 ounces) tuna fish in oil, drained and roughly flaked

2 hard-cooked eggs, shelled and sliced or quartered

1 can (2 ounces) anchovy fillets, drained

salt and freshly ground black pepper

capers and black olives, to garnish

For the dressing

6 tablespoons extra virgin olive oil

2 tablespoons white wine vinegar or lemon juice

2 garlic cloves, crushed

½ teaspoon Dijon mustard

2 tablespoons chopped fresh basil

1 Whisk all the ingredients for the dressing together, season with salt and pepper and let infuse while you make the salad.

2 Cook the pasta in plenty of boiling salted water according to the manufacturer's instructions. Drain well and set aside to cool.

3 Trim the green beans and blanch them in boiling salted water for 3 minutes. Drain, then refresh in cold water.

4 Slice or quarter the tomatoes and arrange on the base of a bowl. Moisten with a little dressing and cover with a quarter of the basil leaves. Then cover with the beans. Moisten with a little more dressing and cover with a third of the remaining basil.

5 Cover with the pasta tossed in a little more dressing, half the remaining basil and the roughly flaked tuna.

6 Arrange the sliced eggs on top. Finally, scatter over the anchovy fillets, capers and black olives. Pour on the remaining dressing and garnish with the remaining basil. Serve immediately. Do not be tempted to chill this salad—all the flavor will be dulled.

COOK'S TIP

Olives marinated in oil flavored with garlic, herbs and lemon peel would add an extra-special touch to this salad. Choose plump, black olives that are fully ripened. Marinated olives are available at large supermarkets and delicatessens, or you could prepare them yourself.

Avocado and Smoked Fish Salad

Avocado and smoked fish make an excellent combination and, flavored with herbs and spices, create a delectable salad.

INGREDIENTS

Serves 4

4 tablespoons (½ stick) butter

½ onion, finely sliced

1 teaspoon mustard seeds

8 ounces smoked mackerel, flaked

2 tablespoons chopped fresh cilantro

2 firm tomatoes, skinned and chopped

1 tablespoon lemon juice

salt and freshly ground black pepper

For the salad

2 avocado pears

½ cucumber

1 tablespoon lemon juice

2 firm tomatoes

1 green chili

1 Melt the butter in a frying pan, add the sliced onion and mustard seeds and fry for about 5 minutes, until the onion is soft, but not colored.

2 Add the fish, cilantro leaves, tomatoes and lemon juice and cook over low heat for 2–3 minutes. Remove from the heat and set aside to cool.

3 Make the salad. Peel and thinly slice the avocado pears and slice the cucumber. Put into a bowl and sprinkle with the lemon juice.

4 Slice the tomatoes. Seed and finely chop the chili.

5 Place the fish mixture in the center of a serving plate.

6 Arrange the avocado pears, cucumber and tomatoes around the fish. Alternatively, spoon a quarter of the fish mixture onto each of 4 serving plates and divide the avocados, cucumber and tomatoes equally. Sprinkle with the chopped chili and a little salt and pepper and serve.

Tuna and Bean Salad

This substantial salad makes a good light meal and can be assembled quickly from canned ingredients.

INGREDIENTS

Serves 4–6

1 can (14 ounces) cannellini or borlotti
  beans

2 cans (7 ounces each) tuna, drained

¼ cup extra virgin olive oil

2 tablespoons fresh lemon juice

1 tablespoon chopped fresh parsley

3 scallions, thinly sliced

salt and freshly ground black pepper

1 Pour the beans into a large strainer and rinse under cold water. Drain well. Place in a serving dish.

2 Break the tuna into fairly large flakes and arrange over the beans in the serving dish.

3 In a small bowl make the dressing by combining the oil with the lemon juice. Season with salt and pepper and stir in the parsley. Mix well. Pour onto the beans and tuna.

4 Sprinkle with the sliced scallion. Toss the salad well before serving.

Thai Seafood Salad

This unusual seafood salad with chili, lemon grass and fish sauce is light and refreshing.

INGREDIENTS

Serves 4

8 ounces ready-prepared squid

8 ounces raw tiger shrimp

8 scallops, shelled

8 ounces firm white fish

2–3 tablespoons olive oil

small mixed lettuce leaves and cilantro
    sprigs, to serve

For the dressing

2 small fresh red chilies, seeded and
    finely chopped

2-inch piece lemon grass, finely chopped

2 fresh kaffir lime leaves, shredded

2 tablespoons Thai fish sauce

2 shallots, thinly sliced

2 tablespoons lime juice

2 tablespoons rice vinegar

2 teaspoons superfine sugar

1 Prepare the seafood. Slit open the squid bodies, cut into square pieces, then score the flesh in a crisscross pattern with a sharp knife. Halve the tentacles, if necessary. Peel and devein the shrimp. Remove the dark beard-like fringe and tough muscle from the scallops. Cube the white fish.

2 Heat a wok or large frying pan until hot. Add the oil and swirl it around, then add the shrimp and stir-fry for 2–3 minutes, until pink. Transfer to a large bowl. Stir-fry the squid and scallops for 1–2 minutes, until opaque. Remove and add to the shrimp. Stir-fry the white fish for 2–3 minutes. Remove and add to the cooked seafood. Reserve any juices.

3 Put all the dressing ingredients in a small bowl with the reserved juices from the wok or frying pan and mix well.

4 Pour the dressing over the seafood and toss gently. Arrange the greens and cilantro sprigs on 4 individual plates, then spoon the seafood on top. Serve immediately.

Eggplant Salad with Dried Shrimp

An appetizing and unusual salad that you will find yourself making over and over again.

INGREDIENTS

Serves 4–6

2 eggplant

1 tablespoon oil

2 tablespoons dried shrimp, soaked
   and drained

1 tablespoon coarsely chopped garlic

2 tablespoons freshly squeezed lime juice

1 teaspoon brown sugar

2 tablespoons fish sauce

1 hard-cooked egg, shelled and chopped

4 shallots, finely sliced into rings

cilantro leaves and 2 red chilies, seeded
   and sliced, to garnish

1 Grill or roast the eggplant
  until charred and tender.

2 When the eggplant is cool
  enough to handle, peel off the
skin and slice the flesh.

3 Heat the oil in a small frying
  pan, add the drained shrimp
and garlic and fry for 3–4 minutes,
until golden. Remove from the pan
and set aside.

4 To make the dressing, put the
  lime juice, brown sugar and
fish sauce in a small bowl and
whisk together.

5 To serve, arrange the eggplant
  on a serving dish. Top with the
egg, shallots and dried shrimp
mixture. Drizzle on the dressing
and garnish with the cilantro
leaves and red chilies.

C O O K ' S   T I P

For an interesting variation, try
using salted ducks' or quails'
eggs, cut in half, instead of
chopped hens' eggs.

Seafood Salad with Fragrant Herbs

This tasty medley of seafood and noodles is a meal in itself.

INGREDIENTS

Serves 4–6

1 cup fish stock or water

12 ounces squid, cleaned and cut into rings

12 raw jumbo shrimp, peeled and deveined

12 scallops, cleaned

2 ounces bean thread noodles, soaked in
   warm water for 30 minutes

½ cucumber, cut into thin sticks

1 stalk lemon grass, finely chopped

2 kaffir lime leaves, finely shredded

2 shallots, finely sliced

juice of 1–2 limes

2 tablespoons fish sauce

2 tablespoons chopped scallion

2 tablespoons cilantro leaves

12–15 mint leaves, roughly torn

4 red chilies, seeded and sliced

cilantro sprigs, to garnish

1 Pour the fish stock into a medium-size saucepan, set over high heat and bring to a boil.

2 Place each type of seafood individually in the stock and cook for a few minutes. Remove and set aside.

3 Drain the bean thread noodles and cut them into short lengths, about 2 inches long. Combine the noodles with the cooked seafood.

4 Add the cucumber, lemon grass, kaffir lime leaves, shallots, lime juice, fish sauce, scallion, cilantro, mint leaves and chilies and combine well. Serve garnished with the cilantro sprigs.

Pomelo Salad

Pomelo is a large, pear-shaped fruit that resembles a grapefruit.

INGREDIENTS

Serves 4-6

2 tablespoons vegetable oil

4 shallots, finely sliced

2 garlic cloves, finely sliced

1 large pomelo

1 tablespoon roasted peanuts

4 ounces cooked peeled shrimp

4 ounces cooked crab meat

10–12 small mint leaves

2 scallions, finely sliced

2 red chilies, seeded and finely sliced

cilantro leaves, to garnish

shredded fresh coconut (optional)

For the dressing

2 tablespoons fish sauce

1 tablespoon brown sugar

2 tablespoons lime juice

1 Make the dressing. Whisk together the fish sauce, brown sugar and lime juice and set aside.

2 Heat the oil in a small frying pan, add the shallots and garlic and fry for 3–4 minutes, until they are golden. Remove from the pan and set aside.

3 Peel the pomelo and break the flesh into small pieces, taking care to remove any membranes.

4 Coarsely grind the peanuts, then combine with the pomelo flesh, shrimp, crab meat, mint leaves and the fried shallot mixture. Toss the salad in the dressing and serve sprinkled with the scallions, red chilies, cilantro leaves and shredded coconut, if using.

Shrimp Salad with Curry Dressing

Curry spices add an unexpected twist to this salad. Warm flavors combine especially well with sweet shrimp and grated apple.

INGREDIENTS

Serves 4

1 ripe tomato

½ head iceberg lettuce, shredded

1 small onion

1 small bunch fresh cilantro

1 tablespoon lemon juice

1 pound cooked peeled shrimp

1 apple, peeled

salt

8 whole cooked shrimp, 8 lemon wedges and 4 sprigs fresh cilantro, to garnish

For the dressing

5 tablespoons mayonnaise

1 teaspoon mild curry paste

1 tablespoon ketchup

2 tablespoons water

1 To peel the tomato, pierce the skin with a knife and immerse in boiling water for 20 seconds. Drain and cool under running water. Peel off the skin. Halve the tomato, push the seeds out with your thumb and discard them. Cut the flesh into large dice.

2 Finely shred the lettuce, onion and cilantro. Add the tomato, moisten with lemon juice and season with salt.

3 To make the dressing, combine the mayonnaise, curry paste and ketchup in a small bowl. Add the water to thin the dressing and season to taste with salt.

4 Combine the shrimp with the dressing. Quarter and core the apple and grate into the mixture.

5 Distribute the shredded lettuce and onion mixture between 4 plates or bowls. Pile the shrimp mixture in the center of each and garnish with 2 whole shrimp, 2 lemon wedges and a sprig of cilantro.

COOK'S TIP

Fresh cilantro is inclined to wilt if it is not kept in water. Store it in the refrigerator, in a jar of water covered with a plastic bag, and it will stay fresh for several days.

Shrimp and Pasta Salad with Green Dressing

Anchovies need a nice strong dressing to match their flavor.

Serves 4-6

4 anchovy fillets, drained

¼ cup milk

8 ounces squid

1 tablespoon chopped capers

1 tablespoon chopped gherkins

1–2 garlic cloves, crushed

⅔ cup plain yogurt

2–3 tablespoons mayonnaise

squeeze of lemon juice

1 small bunch watercress, chopped finely

2 tablespoons chopped fresh parsley

2 tablespoons chopped fresh basil

12 ounces fusilli (pasta spirals)

12 ounces cooked peeled shrimp

salt and freshly ground black pepper

1 Put the anchovies into a small bowl and cover with the milk. Let soak for 10 minutes. Pull the heads off the squid and remove and discard the quills. Peel the outer speckled skin from the bodies and rinse well. Cut into ¼-inch rings. Cut the tentacles from the heads, rinse under cold water and cut into ¼-inch slices.

2 To make the dressing, mix the capers, gherkins, garlic, yogurt, mayonnaise, lemon juice and fresh herbs in a bowl. Drain and chop the anchovies. Add to the dressing with the seasoning.

3 Drop the squid rings and tentacles into a large pan of boiling salted water. Lower the heat and simmer for 1–2 minutes (do not overcook or the squid will become tough). Remove with a slotted spoon. Cook the pasta in the same water according to the instructions on the package. Drain thoroughly.

4 Mix the shrimp and squid into the dressing in a large bowl. Add the pasta, toss and serve immediately. Alternatively, let cool and serve as a salad.

Index